A GROSSET ALL-COLOR GUIDE

SEA BIRDS

BY DAVID SAUNDERS
Illustrated by Ken Lilly

GROSSET & DUNLAP
A NATIONAL GENERAL COMPANY
Publishers ▪ New York

CONTENTS

INTRODUCTION

The name sea bird is a vague term; just what species of birds may be classed under it depends on an individual's own ideas and opinions. Most people would agree, however, that the sea birds of the world belong to four separate major groups, or orders, of birds.

The order Sphenisciformes contains the penguins. The Procellariiformes includes the albatrosses, storm petrels and related species. The Pelecaniformes contains the gannets, pelicans and several other closely related families. Finally, the Charadriiformes, a large order, contains many diverse families, including the jaegers, gulls, terns and auks.

The four orders of sea birds are subdivided into only a few families containing relatively few species, although many have enormous populations, with some colonies containing millions of birds. Of the approximately 8,600 species of birds known today, only 285 are classified as sea birds, and some of these are found in inland waters more than at sea. Land birds, in contrast, are much more widely represented, being classified into 28 different orders, many of which can be divided into numerous suborders and families. While it is likely that a few more new and obscure species of land bird may be discovered hidden in the jungles of South America or the interior of Asia, it is not expected that any new sea bird species will be found.

The four orders into which the world's sea birds are classified are divided into 15 families; in contrast, there are 140 families of land birds.

The single family of Sphenisciformes—the penguins

The Sphenisciformes includes a single family, the Spheniscidae, or penguins, found only in the Southern Hemisphere, though one species reaches the tropics around the Galapagos Islands.

The Procellariiformes are divided into four families. The family Diomedeidae contains the albatrosses, which, except for three North Pacific species, are all birds living in southern oceans, rarely wandering into the North Atlantic. Two families, the Hydrobatidae and the Procellariidae, contain the storm petrels and shearwaters, the vast majority of which

The four families of Procellariiformes—the albatrosses, petrels, shearwaters and diving petrels

inhabit the Southern Hemisphere, particularly the South Pacific. The four diving petrels of the family Pelecanoididae are all restricted to southern oceans.

The Pelecaniformes are divided into six families, of which five are sea birds: the Phaethontidae, or tropic-birds; the Pelecanidae, or pelicans; the Sulidae, or gannets; the Phalacrocoracidae, or cormorants; and the Fregatidae, or frigatebirds. Like the diving petrels, the Pelecaniformes are mostly concentrated in the southern regions.

The Charadriiformes contains 17 families, of which five are sea birds. The Stercorariidae, a small family, contains

The five sea bird families of Pelecaniformes—the tropic-birds, pelicans, gannets, cormorants and frigate-birds

the jaegers. The gulls and terns are often grouped together as the Laridae, but in this book the terns are treated separately as the Sternidae. The latter are distributed fairly evenly throughout the world; the gulls, on the other hand, are best represented in northern regions, although they have spread to many other areas. The three species of skimmer—the Rynchopidae—are all tropical birds. The auk family, the Alcidae, is restricted to northern waters, where its representatives take the ecological place of the penguins and diving petrels of the Southern Hemisphere. Included among the Alcidae are the true auks, the murres, the guillemots, the puffins, the auklets and the murrelets.

The five sea bird families of Charadriiformes—the jaegers, gulls, terns, skimmers and auks

DISTRIBUTION OF SEA BIRDS

Considering that the oceans account for about 70 percent of the surface area of the globe, the number of sea bird species is surprisingly small. On the other hand, some of the most numerous birds in the world, in terms of sheer numbers within a species, are probably the sea birds. Charles Darwin, for example, wrote in the *Origin of Species* that he believed the Northern Fulmar *(Fulmarus glacialis)* to be the most numerous bird species in the world. More recent studies have shown that this is not the case, but that this title should probably be awarded to another member of the storm petrel group, Wilson's Petrel *(Oceanites oceanicus)*. It is, however, very difficult to estimate the population of some sea bird species, especially those which come ashore only to breed.

Some large areas of the oceans are virtually devoid of bird life and are in effect 'avian deserts'. These are generally in regions where the circulation of wind and currents is such that a zone free of any movement is created. One such area is the Sargasso Sea. The absence of turbulence

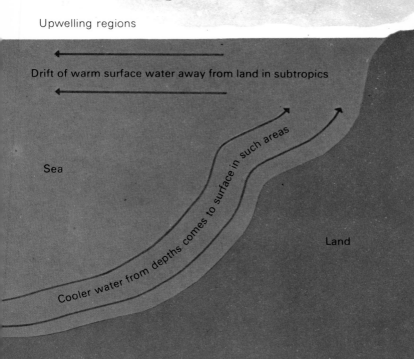

Upwelling regions

Drift of warm surface water away from land in subtropics

Sea

Cooler water from depths comes to surface in such areas

Land

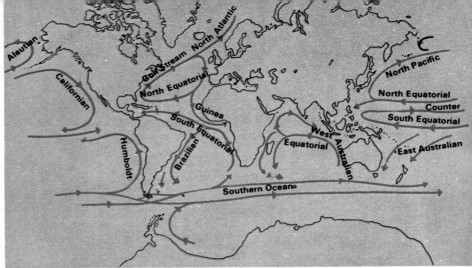

Ocean currents

means that mineral salts, if present, are not brought up to the surface-water layers. Without these nutrients plankton cannot form, so without this primary link in the food chain there is a corresponding absence of fish and the birds which prey on them for their chief source of food.

The rotation of the earth causes currents to flow clockwise in the Northern Hemisphere and counterclockwise in the Southern. The effect of this is to bring water from one region to the coasts of another, where a vertical mixing will take place as the water begins to 'pile up'. The same action will take place in the region from which the water has drifted. In this case the deeper layers will be brought to the surface. The effect of all this upwelling and turbulence is to ensure that nutrients are brought to the surface and dispersed. These may be concentrated in some areas by currents, while in others such material will be scanty or nonexistent.

These upwellings occur in well-known places such as in the Canary Current off West Africa and off South America in the Humboldt Current. Such upwellings of cooler water mean that some species can exist much farther north into tropical waters than would otherwise be possible. It is in such plankton-rich areas that the largest communities of sea birds are found.

World map showing sea bird habitats

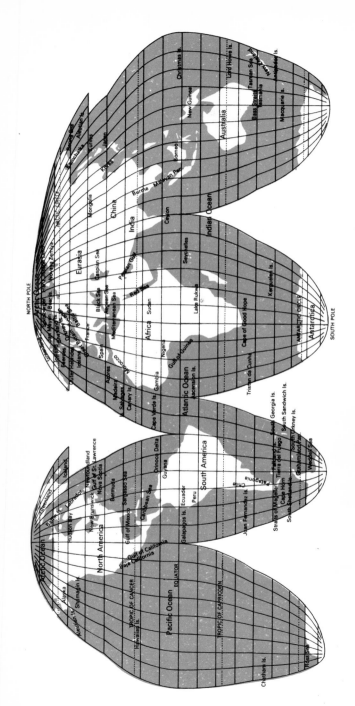

9

The distribution of sea birds varies in the different oceans. The largest concentration is found in the Pacific, where nearly half the species may be seen. Next in order comes the Atlantic, followed by the Indian, Antarctic and Arctic Oceans; the Mediterranean Sea has the fewest number of sea birds.

The distribution of sea birds in an area may be divided into three zones—inshore, offshore and pelagic, at sea. Some species may be confined throughout their range to one or another zone, while others may, for example, be inshore feeders during the breeding season, but otherwise roam the oceans as pelagic species.

Some sea birds may be very restricted in range, while others are found throughout the world. One of the most widespread is the Caspian Tern *(Hydroprogne caspia)*. As can be seen from the accompanying map, this large and handsome species of tern has a wide, though scattered, distribution throughout the world. It is found both on coasts and far inland, and is absent as a breeding species only from South America. The inference from such a widespread and disrupted breeding range is that the Caspian Tern is an ancient species. Its breeding range may have been larger and more continuous than it is today; disturbance by man probably accounts for its present discontinuous distribution.

Other sea birds besides the Caspian Tern have wide ranges, though, unlike some land birds, none seems to have been introduced into new areas. The Roseate Tern *(Sterna dougallii)* is another widespread tern, though it, too, does not nest in South America. Unlike the Caspian Tern, the Roseate very much prefers coasts and islands for breeding. Even though it is widespread, it is not a very abundant species.

Some species, such as the Black-headed Gull *(Larus ridibundus)*, may be very widespread in one region, in this case Europe and Asia, but only a rare visitor elsewhere. Others may breed in one zone, yet travel vast distances during the off-season to feed in another. The Wilson's Petrel, for example, breeds in the Antarctic regions and flies north into the North Pacific and Atlantic during the polar winter.

Although a number of sea bird species are wide-ranging and almost universal in their choice of breeding and feeding

Caspian Tern and map showing its distribution

areas, others are very restricted. The Audouin's Gull (L. audouinii) is a typical example. As can be seen from the map, it is found only on a scattering of islands within the Mediterranean zone and the actual number of pairs is little more than 1,000. It is a species which seems to be vanishing as breeding areas become more prone to disturbance. Another possible danger to its continued existence is predation of its eggs and chicks by other gull species.

The Mediterranean Black-headed Gull (L. melanocephalus) must also be considered to be a vanishing species. It is restricted to the eastern Mediterranean and the Black Sea, although there is a report by the explorer Sven Hedinn of an isolated breeding population in central Asia. Unlike Audouin's Gull, this species does wander farther afield and appears almost annually in Great Britain, among other places.

The Waved Albatross (Diomedea irrorata), although found nesting only on one island in the Galapagos Islands off Ecuador, wanders far across the Pacific when young or during the off-season. Another species restricted entirely to the Galapagos Islands is the Flightless Cormorant (Nannopterum harrisi). Unlike the albatross, the cormorant does not wander from its breeding islands but stays within the same region throughout its life. Since it does not need to fly, this bird has lost the use of its wings.

When birds are so restricted in their breeding range there

Distribution of Audouin's Gull

Audouin's Gull

is a danger that they could quickly become extinct. For example, the Great Auk *(Pinguinus impennis)*, a restricted species in the sense that it was flightless, was bludgeoned into extinction to satisfy man's greed. In these hopefully more enlightened days this will not be allowed to happen again. However, this is no safeguard against changes in an ocean current or the occurrence of a natural disaster which might so alter the ecology of an area that a species of a restricted nature could quickly be lost to the world.

Many sea bird species may be divided into subspecies; some into several. A subspecies is one which may be distinguished from other populations of the same species. Because of differences of opinion among taxonomists the number of subspecies is constantly changing, leading to some confusion

13

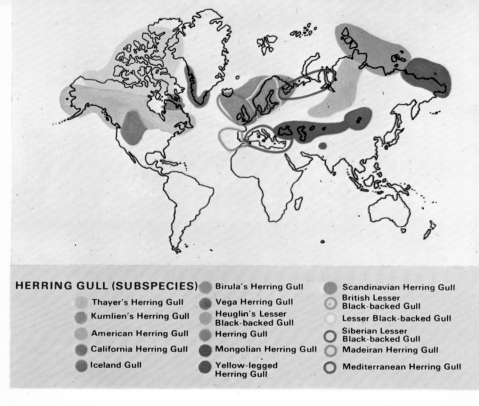

HERRING GULL (SUBSPECIES)

- Thayer's Herring Gull
- Kumlien's Herring Gull
- American Herring Gull
- California Herring Gull
- Iceland Gull

- Birula's Herring Gull
- Vega Herring Gull
- Heuglin's Lesser Black-backed Gull
- Herring Gull
- Mongolian Herring Gull
- Yellow-legged Herring Gull

- Scandinavian Herring Gull
- British Lesser Black-backed Gull
- Lesser Black-backed Gull
- Siberian Lesser Black-backed Gull
- Madeiran Herring Gull
- Mediterranean Herring Gull

Distribution of the Herring Gull and its subspecies

among ornithologists. In this book, therefore, there will be few references to subspecific forms.

An example of the sort of chaos that can result may be seen in the cases of the Herring Gull *(Larus argentatus)* and Lesser Black-backed Gull *(L. fuscus)*. In both the New World and the Old there are a number of other gulls, sometimes considered as full species, sometimes only with a sub-specific rank, which come into the same grouping.

Starting with Birula's Herring *(L. argentatus birulai)*, a central Siberian bird, there are two chains of subspecies that circle the polar basin to meet in overlapping links. Neighboring populations of Herring Gulls are not too different from one another, varying mainly in shade of color of plumage, bill and legs. Most populations seem to have distinct breeding areas, though where they overlap, hybrids occur. However, at each end of the chain the differences become marked; in western Europe, for example, the Herring Gull is readily distinguishable from the Lesser Black-backed Gull. In this overlap zone the two gulls behave as different species. They are different not only in color, but in their habits as well. However, interbreeding between the two has been recorded on several occasions.

The Herring Gull tends to be a sedentary bird, normally not wandering great distances from its natal area. It often breeds on cliffs and cliff slopes as well as on level ground. The Lesser Black-backed Gull, easily distinguished by its darker mantle and yellow legs, is a migratory species. Most leave their northern quarters during the winter months for Iberia and West Africa. Their breeding colonies, which are re-occupied during February and March, are usually on more level ground, often far inland. In feeding habits the species differ in some respects; for instance, the Herring Gull is much more of a scavenger.

(Top to bottom) Iceland Gull, Herring Gull, Yellow-legged Gull, Lesser Black-backed Gull

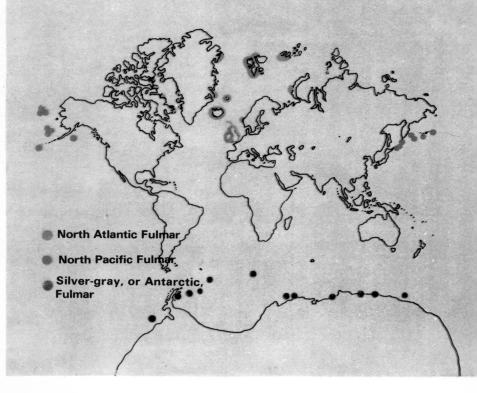

North Atlantic Fulmar

North Pacific Fulmar

Silver-gray, or Antarctic, Fulmar

Map showing Fulmar distribution

In any species there may be marked changes in size from one part of its range to another. This phenomenon is called a cline, a term first used by Sir Julian Huxley in 1939. Individuals from either end of the range may differ so·considerably from one another that they are given subspecific rank. The changes throughout the range may not be gradual or even, but rather occur in a series of jumps or steps.

Three 'rules' have been formulated that help explain clinical variation. Bergmann's rule states that 'body size tends to be larger in the cooler parts of the total range and smaller in the warmer parts'. Thus animals in the far north will be larger than those of the same species further south.

Allen's rule states that 'extensions of the body (in birds, chiefly bills) tend to be longer in the warmer parts of the

(Top to bottom)
Silver-gray, or
Antarctic, Fulmar,
North Pacific Fulmar,
North Atlantic Fulmar

total range and shorter in the cooler parts'. The larger-bodied animals in the north have less surface area in relation to weight, so that heat loss is not so rapid. As a further adaptation, appendages which might lose heat in the north are also reduced in size.

Gloger's rule states that 'in a more humid region animals will be darker pigmented than those in the dry areas'.

There are also clines in such things as bill shape. A good example of this is found in the fulmars. Birds from the Antarctic, known as Silver-gray Fulmars, have slender bills, while in the North Pacific, bills are slightly larger. Crossing into the Arctic/Atlantic area, we find bills among the North Atlantic Fulmars which are even stouter, particularly in the northeastern part of the region.

THE SEA BIRD GROUPS

Penguins

Few people visiting a zoo or looking at pictures in a book see these birds and fail to be captivated by them. Perhaps this is because we tend to see in them various human characteristics, particularly their upright stance and inquisitive nature.

Eighteen species of penguins have been described, all of which are restricted to the Southern Hemisphere, though by no means to the polar regions. The largest of all is the Emperor Penguin *(Aptenodytes forsteri),* which in peak condition can weigh as much as 90 pounds, though it normally averages 66 pounds, and is nearly 4 feet in height. The other species range in size down to the Little Penguin *(Eudyptula minor)* of Australia and New Zealand, also known as the Fairy Penguin and the Little Blue Penguin.

Fossil remains, again restricted to the Southern Hemisphere, show that larger species existed at one time. At least one of these, now named *Pachydyptes ponderous,* stood about 5 feet high. Why this species and others which we know from their fossil records died out is impossible to tell. Those remains so far discovered seem to indicate a bone structure and general appearance similar to that of species alive today. Information about earlier members of the order is still not available, though perhaps as a guide we may turn to the auks of the Northern Hemisphere and the diving petrels of the Southern. Members of both groups use their wings as paddles under water; the wings are stunted so that they need to be flapped vigorously during flight. Even in calm weather, take-off from the sea is exceedingly difficult.

Penguins, their powers of flight lost long ago, and their wings flattened to strong narrow flippers, have adapted themselves even further to their environment. Their torpedo-like bodies can be projected through the water at speeds of up to ten knots, the tail and feet being used as rudders. Quite often the mode of travel is by 'porpoising', the bird breaking clear of the surface while inhaling air, then diving beneath to swim for several more yards. On land, penguins spend most of their time in an upright position, though in snow some species occasionally flop down on their bellies and 'toboggan', using their feet and flippers to propel them.

Relative sizes of Miocene penguin, Man, Emperor, Adelie
and Little Penguins

6

5

4

3

2

1

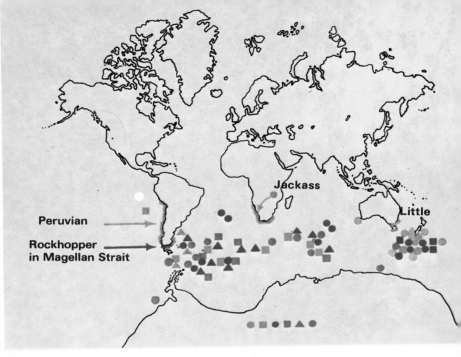

Peruvian

Rockhopper
in Magellan Strait

Jackass

Little

Distribution of various penguin species

The plumage of penguins, unlike that of most birds, covers the whole body and is very short and dense. The longest feathers, belonging to the Emperor Penguin, barely reach 3½ inches in length, while in some of the smaller species they do not exceed 1 inch. Beneath this dense overcoat of feathers lies a thick layer of blubber, or fat, which not only provides extra insulation for the body, but is a storage organ for both food and water.

Penguins feed generally on animals caught close to the surface of the sea within easy reach of the shore. The larger species feed on squid, which abound in Antarctic waters, and supplement their diet with fish. Those species which range farther north eat large quantities of small fish; it has been estimated that four-fifths of the food taken by the Jackass, or Black-footed, Penguin (*Spheniscus demersus*) off south-western Africa is of this nature. Each penguin requires about 9 ounces of food a day, so that in a year the population of

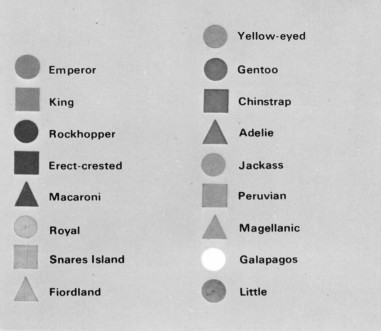

● Emperor		● Yellow-eyed	
		● Gentoo	
■ King		■ Chinstrap	
● Rockhopper		▲ Adelie	
■ Erect-crested		● Jackass	
▲ Macaroni		■ Peruvian	
● Royal		▲ Magellanic	
■ Snares Island		○ Galapagos	
▲ Fiordland		● Little	

Jackass Penguins, numbering some 100,000 birds, may consume 6,000 tons of fish. An increase in human fishing activity in the area could seriously affect these penguins by diminishing their food supply.

Krill, the name given to the shrimp-like crustaceans *Euphausia superba*, which in their countless billions stain the surface of Antarctic seas red in certain seasons, provides an abundant source of food. The droppings of birds which feed on these organisms are also stained bright red. With man's wanton destruction of the great whales, the amount of krill now available has vastly increased; this may account for the colonization of new areas by the Chinstrap Penguin *(Pygoscelis antarctica)*.

A possible serious menace to penguin colonies is disturbance by man, which can even take place in the far frozen south unless special care is taken. With the advent of tourism in the Antarctic, disturbance of penguin colonies must be avoided at all costs.

The two species of Penguin which extend their range farthest south are the Emperor Penguin and the Adelie Penguin *(P. adeliae)*, the latter named by the French explorer Dumont d' Urville in honor of his wife, Adélie.

The Emperor is restricted to the coasts of the Antarctic continent, while the Adelie, although found on the mainland, also extends northward to the South Shetland, South Orkney and South Sandwich Islands.

Some 20 or so colonies of Emperor Penguins are known, the largest being on Coulman Island in the Ross Sea, where 100,000 birds congregate, a fifth of the world's total. The first Emperor Penguins were caught by members of Sir James Clark Ross's expedition in 1842, but it was not until 1902 that the first breeding colony was discovered. This was found on Cape Crozier by the men of Captain Scott's 'Discovery' expedition, who were amazed to see young birds in down, meaning that hatching had taken place during the polar night.

At that time penguins were considered to be very primitive birds and it was thought that a study of chick embryos might lead to information concerning the origin of birds. Consequently, on Scott's second polar expedition in 1910 Edward Wilson, 'Birdie' Bowers and Apsley Cherry-Garrard manhauled their sledges under appalling conditions through the darkness and biting winds of the Antarctic winter to Cape Crozier. For all this, the embryos which were brought back on examination revealed little which was not already known.

Only the male Emperor Penguin incubates the single egg, which takes 64 days to hatch. During this time the females are on the open sea, which may be up to 100 miles away across the ice. The chicks are fed first by the males on a crop secretion, after which the females take over while their mates go to sea. Toward the end of the fledging period, both parents assist in the feeding, though the chicks leave to fend for themselves before they are fully grown. At this stage the juveniles congregate at the edge of the ice shelf, often commencing their northern journey on an ice floe, until they are able to enter the sea after assuming their final coat of feathers.

Emperor Penguin and chick (left), Adelie Penguin and chick (right)

King Penguin

In the sub-Antarctic zone, a region of remote islands and howling westerly gales, several other penguin species are found. The largest of these is the King Penguin *(Aptenodytes patagonica)*, a familiar figure in zoos throughout the world. It is half the weight of its close relative the Emperor Penguin, though only 1 foot less in height.

The nesting site of this species is usually on bare, muddy ground close to the shore. A single egg is laid and both parents share the incubation, which is carried out with the egg balanced on the upper surface of the adult's feet. The incubation period is about 54 days, after which both parents feed the chick, which grows rapidly throughout the southern autumn. Clad in its thick eiderdown, it faces the long winter at the nest site, living on stored fat reserves and receiving occasional feedings. During this period the smaller and weaker chicks die, while even the healthy ones lose half their autumn weight. With the onset of spring, feeding recommences and

Chinstrap Penguin (top) and Gentoo Penguin (right) in pursuit of fish

the chicks, now molting their brown down, begin to leave the colony. If parents have lost an egg or chick they will lay again during the spring, while those that have been more successful will wait until the following season. Many will, therefore, only breed twice in three years, laying eggs early in one season and late in another.

Other sub-Antarctic species include the Gentoo Penguin *(P. papua)*, which occurs in several subspecies throughout its range, and the Chinstrap Penguin. Gentoos are mild-natured; the Chinstraps, belligerent and noisy.

Both species breed in huge, crowded colonies, nesting close together. Nests are built from accumulations of stone and other debris, while Gentoos living farther north can afford the comparative luxury of clumps of tussock grass. Two white eggs are usually laid and both parents take part in the incubation, which lasts about 35 days.

Other penguin species are encountered farther north,

among them the six members of the genus *Eudyptes*. All have distinct yellow crests, the arrangement of which provides an identification guide to the species involved.

Four of the species have a somewhat restricted range: the Royal Penguin *(E. schlegeli)* is found only on Macquarie Island; the Erect-crested Penguin *(E. sclateri)* lives on the Antipodes, Bounty and Campbell Islands; the Snares Island Penguin *(E. robustus)* is restricted to the archipelago of the same name south of New Zealand, while the Fiordland Penguin *(E. pachyrhynchus)* resides on the deeply indented coast at the southern end of South Island, New Zealand. The other two species are much more wide-ranging. The Macaroni Penguin *(E. chrysolophus)* is found southward in the subpolar regions, while the Rockhopper *(E. crestatus)* extends as far north as the Falkland Islands and Tristan da Cunha.

The members of this group spend much of their time away from the nesting colonies, which may be deserted for up to five months of the year. The birds congregate for nesting in vast avian metropolises—up to 2,000,000 Royal Penguins nest on Macquarie Island; there are also large numbers of nonbreeding young birds present, as the birds mature between five and seven years of age. Two eggs are laid but only the larger, second egg is incubated. Both sexes take part in the incubation, which lasts for 35 days.

The genus *Eudyptula* includes two species confined to the Australasian region. The Little Penguin *(Eudyptula minor)* is found as far north as Sydney, Australia. It nests in burrows and crevices, even under coastal bungalows, and may walk up to a mile inland to find a suitable site. Two, sometimes three, eggs are laid and incubation is carried out by both parents. The chicks hatch between the 33rd and 40th day and are guarded by each parent in turn, the off-duty bird bringing back food at night. Of similar habits is the White-flippered Penguin *(Eudyptula albosignata)*, which is restricted to the South Island of New Zealand. Another warmer-climate species is the Yellow-eyed Penguin *(Megadyptes antipodes)* of southern New Zealand.

Jackass Penguin (top), Little Penguin (bottom left) and White-flippered Penguin (right)

Four species of penguins, all belonging to the genus *Spheniscus*, range farther north than any other species. The Magellanic Penguin *(S. magellanicus)* inhabits the bleak coasts and islands around the southern tip of South America, including the Falkland Islands. Still farther north, the Peruvian, or Humboldt, Penguin *(S. homboldti)* makes use of the cool, food-rich waters of the Humboldt Current and ranges to within five degrees of the Equator. Off southwestern Africa, the Jackass, or Black-footed, Penguin thrives in large colonies because of the cool Benegula Current.

The rarest of all is the Galapagos Penguin *(S. mendiculus)*, restricted, as its name suggests, to the Galapagos Islands. Here some 500 pairs reside on Albemarle and Narborough Islands, within a degree and a half of the Equator. Their very existence in the area is dependent on the cool currents swinging out from the South American shore, a continuation of those which

Magellanic Penguin (left) and Peruvian Penguin (right)

enable the Peruvian Penguin to come so far north. The Galapagos Penguin seeks rock crevices and caverns as nesting sites, generally in sheltered bays close to the water's edge. It usually lays two eggs.

The other three species also nest in burrows and crevices, normally laying two eggs. The incubation period is about four weeks; the Jackass Penguin may feed its chicks for up to three months.

Two species of penguins are, or were, important producers of guano, the nitrogen-rich dung accumulated at large sea bird colonies. Whole islands off Peru have been stripped haphazardly of this important asset by man, so that the nest sites of some species which burrow in the beds of accumulated droppings, notably the Peruvian Penguin, were destroyed. As much as 5,500 tons of guano produced by the Jackass Penguin is still taken annually from the South African region.

Galapagos Penguin under water

Wandering Albatross in flight and on land

Albatrosses

The 13 species of albatrosses which exist at the present time are all truly pelagic birds, notable for their large size and powers of flight. They occur in two genera — *Diomedea*, containing 11 species, and *Phoebetria,* with two. The order Procellarii-formes, to which albatrosses belong, also includes the smaller shearwaters and petrels described later.

An albatross is a stoutly built bird which on the ground looks rather ugly, a fact due in part to its characteristically large head and bill. The latter may reach up to 6 inches in length; the tip is hooked and the entire bill is covered by horny plates instead of the single sheath that most birds possess. The sexes are generally alike, except in the case of the Wandering

Albatross *(D. exulans),* where the female has a dark crown cap. Albatrosses are ungainly when ashore, owing to the fact that their short legs are placed far back on the body, so that they waddle rather than walk.

Probably because of this clumsiness when on land, sailors have given them names like 'goony- or gony-birds', 'gony' being an English dialect name for 'simple person'. Other names include 'mollymawk' or 'mollyhawk', a term which sometimes includes other maritime species like jaegers and immature gulls. These names seem to be derived from the Dutch *mollemuck, mol* meaning foolish and *mok* a gull.

The long wings of the albatross enable it to spend a great part of its life at sea, gliding for what seems like hours on almost motionless wings. The largest species, the Wandering Albatross, has a wingspan of 12 feet, the largest wingspan of any bird, though it is not the largest bird in overall dimensions. Using its broad feet, which project beyond the tail as a rudder, an albatross can glide as swiftly across the wind as with it. The troughs and crests of the waves create air currents that the birds utilize to gain height swiftly; then they swoop low to repeat the procedure. As they often live in areas where strong winds are prevalent, albatrosses are able to use this gliding ability to a remarkable degree. If the wind drops, a somewhat labored flapping flight is adopted.

Distribution of various albatrosses

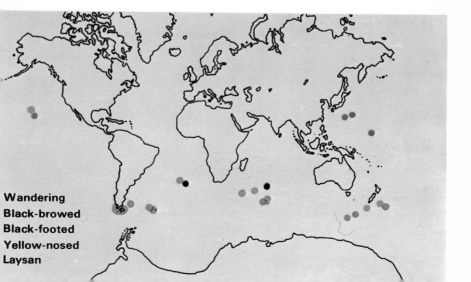

Wandering
Black-browed
Black-footed
Yellow-nosed
Laysan

Albatrosses usually form colonies when nesting; some congregations may be very large. The nests may be nothing more than depressions in the ground, though some species accumulate mounds of vegetable debris. A single egg is laid that is mainly white with a few darker speckles.

Both sexes take part in the incubation, which generally lasts about 70 days. The chicks are already covered in down when hatched and during the early stages are brooded continuously. They are fed on regurgitated fish brought back to the nest by both parents, and on this rich diet, growth is rapid. A three-month-old Wandering Albatross chick, for example, may weigh as much as an adult. By this age, the chicks are being left unguarded and feeding becomes somewhat erratic. There is evidence to suggest that the parent birds may wander tremendous distances while still feeding a chick. A parent from a colony in South Georgia, an island off the tip of South America, was recognized some 2,640 miles away, while in the North Pacific, albatrosses with small chicks have been recovered 2,000 miles from their colony. When left alone, the young birds defend themselves by spitting out stomach oil at any intruder approaching too close. This habit is also exhibited by related species such as the fulmars.

The length of the breeding season in the smaller albatrosses is about five months, after which the chicks finally make their own way to the sea. The young of the Wandering Albatross and the Royal Albatross (D. epomophora) may remain with the adult birds for nearly a year. The chicks of these species finally leave the colony about 11 months after the eggs are laid, when the adults are beginning to gather for another breeding season.

At the beginning of the breeding season albatrosses perform elaborate displays which are communal in some species. In some cases this display may continue during incubation, while some performances have been noted at sea, far from the nesting colony; yearling birds have also been observed taking part in these displays.

Courtship displays of two adult male albatrosses: (top to bottom) threat posture; bill clapping or rattling; swaying gait and sky-pointing; 'dancing' with outstretched wings

Sooty Albatross

Ten species of albatross are found in the Southern Hemisphere. Most breed on remote oceanic islands but sometimes extend farther south into subpolar regions.

The Wandering Albatross breeds in three widely separated areas: in the South Atlantic, on the islands of Inaccessible, Tristan da Cunha and Gough; in the South Indian Ocean, on Kerguelen, Crozets, Prince Edward and Marion Islands; and on the Auckland, Antipodes, Campbell and Macquarie Islands to the south of New Zealand. The total world population has been estimated to be on the order of 100,000 birds.

Two other species, the Yellow-nosed *(D. chlororhynchos)* and Sooty Albatrosses *(P. fusca)*, also nest on Tristan da Cunha. The former closely resembles the Gray-headed Albatross *(D. chrysostoma)*, which nests further south on the islands near Cape Horn. The Yellow-nosed Albatross ranges farther north in the South Atlantic and is one of the species

Buller's Albatross (left) and Gray-headed Albatross (right)

most often seen along the shipping routes in the area.

One of the rarer and less well-known species is Buller's Albatross *(D. bulleri)*, which breeds on the Snares and Chatham Islands off South Island, New Zealand, moving eastward toward Chile and Peru during the winter months.

The food taken by albatrosses is picked off the surface of the sea or from just beneath it. Squids form a large part of the diet of some species, while others eat refuse discarded at sea. For this reason, the Black-footed Albatross *(D. nigripes)* of the North Pacific is known as the feathered pig.

The movements of albatrosses have been studied in certain areas by the use of banding techniques. Large numbers of Wandering Albatrosses have been banded at colonies in South Georgia. Recoveries indicate a dispersal of birds across the oceans rather than a definite migration. Long distances may be traversed; one bird was noted 6,000 miles from its colony.

Laysan Albatross

Three species of albatross are found in North Pacific waters: the Short-tailed *(D. albatrus)*, the Laysan *(D. immutabilis)* and the Black-footed.

All are now very much restricted in their breeding ranges. The Short-tailed Albatross has been on the verge of extinction for some years. Once occurring in large numbers on islands to the south of Japan, vast numbers were killed by fishermen and by those seeking the birds' plumage for the feather industry. Between 1887 and 1903 an estimated 5,000,000 birds were killed on the island of Toroshima in the Izu group, while in 1922–23 almost the whole breeding population of some 3,000 birds was exterminated. Natural hazards in the form of violent volcanic activity further decimated the colony in 1939 and again in 1941. The very survival of the species seems to have been dependent on the return of non-breeders that were away at sea when the eruptions took place. The birds are now protected by the Japanese government; in 1955, 10 pairs were present, 18 in 1958, and 47 birds in 1962.

The Black-footed Albatross is now confined to the Leeward Chain of the Hawaiian Islands. In 1957–58 the world popula-

Short-tailed Albatross

tion of this species was believed to be about 300,000, of which 110,000 nest in any one season.

The Laysan Albatross is also now restricted to the Lee-ward Chain of the Hawaiian Islands, except for a few on Toroshima. The total population in 1957–58 was on the order of 1,500,000 birds, of which 560,000 nest in any one year. The establishment of defense bases on certain Pacific Islands led to a conflict between military requirements and those of the birds. In spite of precautionary measures, however, the bird-strike problem still remains and in one ten-month period, damage to planes cost $83,000.

Black-footed Albatross

Like the penguin family, albatrosses have one representative restricted to the Galapagos Islands: the Waved Albatross *(D. irrorata),* which nests on Hood Island, where there is a fairly stable breeding population of about 3,000 pairs. During the off-season, birds range the Pacific Ocean east to the coasts of Ecuador and Peru and westward to Japanese waters.

The albatrosses of Hood Island nest in scattered groups on the bare ground among thorn bushes and boulders, often at a distance of several hundred yards inland from the cliffs. Landing in a terrain with such obstacles is a hazardous busi-

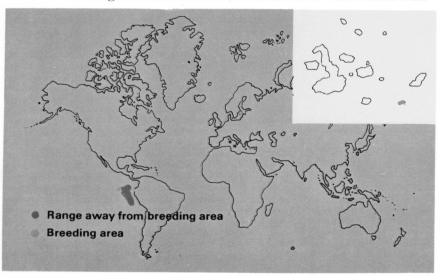

● **Range away from breeding area**

● **Breeding area**

Distribution of Waved Albatross; breeding station on Hood Island in the Galapagos (inset)

ness. During his stay on the island, Dr. J. B. Nelson found two birds which had died from injuries received while landing. Leg and foot wounds were commonplace. Taking off also presents difficulties and many birds are content to plod slowly to the cliff edge before attempting to become airborne.

After hatching, the single chick is brooded by its parents for the first two weeks or so, after which it is left unguarded and seeks shelter beneath nearby bushes. Chicks seem to recognize their returning parents from their distinct call-notes.

Waved Albatross and chick

The Waved Albatross feeds its chick on a regurgitated rich, oily liquid made from food consumed while at sea. This method of feeding enables the birds to roam at will as, unlike many other sea birds, there is no rush to return before the food deteriorates. The chick places its beak, usually sideways, into that of the adult in order to be fed. Prodigious amounts may be given at a single sitting, even as much as four pounds of oil, so that the chick's daily weight fluctuates greatly. Feeding becomes less frequent as the young bird reaches the flying stage—usually when it is about seven months old.

Fossils of extinct albatrosses have been discovered in many areas. One of the most interesting was found in England in the last century; since then, similar remains have been discovered in eastern North America. It seems highly likely that before the climatic and geographical changes which took place during the period of the great Ice Age, albatrosses roamed the North Atlantic. However, they seem to have been unable to recolonize what would appear to be an eminently suitable region for them.

The restriction on their free movement from the South Atlantic northward seems to be the Doldrums—the area of calms—which presents an almost insurmountable barrier for species like the albatrosses. To the west, natural land barriers prevent colonization by the Pacific species.

Occasionally albatrosses are reported in the North Atlantic, but in the past such records were regarded with some scepticism, as it was known that sailors kept the birds as pets during long ocean voyages. It is now many years since sailors indulged in such pursuits but albatrosses are still reported, increasingly so in recent years.

Most reports probably refer to a migratory species, the Black-browed Albatross (D. melanophris). During the southern winter these birds move northward, following the cold currents toward more tropical waters; from time to time they manage to cross the Equator. If enough of these birds were able to reach the North Atlantic there is no reason why they should not establish themselves in the area easily, since the climate is suitable and food available.

There have been several indications that this could happen. Between 1860 and 1894 an albatross was regularly noted in the gannet colony on Mykines Holm in the Faroes, until it was killed by bird hunters. More recently one was seen in a gannet colony on the Westmann Islands, Iceland, and since 1967 one has been seen, to the amazement of many bird-watchers, among the gannets on the Bass Rock, Scotland.

Black-browed Albatross in flight (left) and (below) in foreground of picture with gannets

Wilson's Petrel

Storm petrels

The 22 species of storm petrel are the smallest web-footed sea
birds, similar in size to such land birds as the House Martin
(*Delichon urbica*). In fact, they resemble this species in
general appearance. Most are whitish beneath and dark
above, with pale rumps. The smallest is the Least Storm
Petrel (*Halocyptena microsoma*), some 5 inches in length,
which nests on islands off Baja California. Other species
range in size up to 10 inches in length.

The birds were probably named after St. Peter, because they
seem to walk on the surface of the sea during feeding. They
often follow in the wake of ships, where they pick up items of
food thrown to the surface by the churning propellers; not all
species, however, have this habit. A favorite name among
sailors for these birds is Mother Carey's chickens; this comes
from the words Mater Cara, which is an appellation of the
Blessed Virgin Mary.

Who can say with any degree of certainty which is the most
numerous bird in the world? A number of sea bird species
could lay claim to this title, including Wilson's Petrel
(*Oceanites oceanicus*), which breeds in vast uncountable
colonies at many sites in Antarctica and on sub-Antarctic
islands like Kerguelen and the Falklands.

At the breeding colonies, nests are built in cliff crevices, among boulders, on mountain slopes and in burrows in the peaty soil. These sites are typical, also, of the rest of the family. The colonies are usually visited during the hours of darkness, the day being spent at sea or in the nest chamber. A single white egg is laid and both parents take part in the incubation and feeding of the chick, which is some seven weeks old when it leaves the nest. From those species studied in any detail, it is evident that the storm petrels are several years old before they return to the colonies to breed.

During the southern winter the Wilson's. Petrel moves northward into the main ocean basins, though less into the Pacific than elsewhere. On the east coast of North America, Wilson's Petrel is very common, often coming in close to shore, though it is rarely blown inland. There are few British sightings, though the bird is probably more numerous in that area than the records indicate, for it is frequently seen in the Bay of Biscay.

Characteristic flight of Wilson's Petrel (top right) and pattering on water (right)

The storm petrels are scattered throughout the world's oceans. Some, like the Wilson's Petrel, have a wide distribution, particularly during the winter months; others are much more restricted. Some, like the Gray-backed Storm Petrel *(Garrodia neresis)*, nest in the Antarctic regions and roam throughout the southern oceans, while on the other side of the world the Fork-tailed Petrel *(Oceanodroma furcata)* lives in the North Pacific, with colonies on the island chain of the Kuriles and Aleutians and on the islands off the west coast of North America, as far south as Oregon.

Hornby's Storm Petrel *(O. hornbyi)* breeds high in the Chilean Andes, while Elliot's Storm Petrel *(O. gracilis)* is one of several species restricted to various island archipelagos in the central Pacific Ocean.

Leach's Petrel *(O. leucorhoa)* is a very numerous bird on the eastern coast of North America, breeding in large colonies, perhaps in millions, on islands off the coasts of southern Labrador, Newfoundland, New Brunswick, Nova Scotia and Maine. It is also found, though only in comparatively small

British Storm Petrel (top), and Elliot's Storm Petrel (bottom)

numbers, i.e., several thousand pairs, on several islands off northwestern Britain, in the Faroes—where nesting was first noted in 1934—and on the Westmann Islands. In the North Pacific, the bird's breeding range extends northward from Baja California to Alaska and westward to the Kuriles.

The British Storm Petrel *(Hydrobates pelagicus)* breeds on remote islands and coasts from the Westmann Islands, Iceland, south to the Canary Islands, one of its major strongholds being islands off western Britain. Some of these undoubtedly contain colonies with many thousand birds, but because of the species' nocturnal nature and the difficult terrain in which it often nests, true assessments of the population are hard to come by.

Another widespread species is the White-faced Storm Petrel *(Pelagodroma marina)*, which nests on Tristan da Cunha, the Cape Verde Islands and the Salvages in the Atlantic Ocean, on New Amsterdam and St. Pauls in the southern Indian Ocean, on the Galapagos Islands in the Pacific and at many sites around New Zealand and along the southern coasts of Australia.

Leach's Petrel (top) and Hornby's
Storm Petrel (bottom)

Fulmars

There are six species which are normally classified as fulmars, the largest of which is the Giant Petrel *(Macronectes giganteus);* with a wingspan of 6½ feet, it is more the size of a small albatross. Found on a range of islands encircling the Antarctic continent, the Giant Petrel takes two forms: white in high latitudes, dark in more temperate regions. A formidable bird, it feeds on carcasses washed ashore, but also kills other sea birds such as penguins, gulls and prions.

The Cape Pigeon *(Daption capensis)* also breeds on a range of sites around Antarctica, including the Grahamland Peninsula. Although well known to sailors in southern waters, the first nest was found only in 1903 by members of the Scottish National Antarctic Expedition in South Orkney.

Two other species, the Antarctic Petrel *(Thalassoica antarctica)* and the Snow Petrel *(Pagodroma nivea),* are both restricted to the far south. The latter is almost confined to the great ice barriers and is found farther south than any sea bird except for the Emperor Penguin and Great Skua *(Catharacta skua).*

The Silver-gray, or Antarctic, Fulmar *(Fulmarus glacialoides),* breeding on the Antarctic mainland and offshore islands, is believed to be the stock from which birds crossed into the North Pacific, probably during the Ice Age. Eventually birds passed into the North Atlantic, so that the Northern Fulmar *(F. glacialis)* now occurs in both northern oceans as two subspecies, the North Atlantic and North Pacific Fulmars (see page 16).

In both the Pacific and Atlantic there is a variation in color from light forms through intermediate to darker, or 'blue', forms. In northeastern Canada, Greenland, and northern islands like Novaya Zemlya and Spitzbergen the population is mainly blue. On Bear Island approximately 60 percent are blue, while farther south the bulk of the population is of the pale type. A general rule seems to be that where the sea-water temperature is above freezing in July, the birds are of the light form, with the blue occurring where the sea water is at or below the freezing point. In the Pacific this rule is reversed.

The North Atlantic Fulmar has attracted a good deal of attention from British ornithologists during the present century. In the 17th century, fulmars were known to be nesting

Giant Petrel (top), Cape
Pigeon (bottom left) and Silver-
gray Fulmar (bottom right)

only south of Jan Mayen, on Grimsay off Iceland and on the islands of St. Kilda to the west of the Outer Hebrides. In the years that followed, the birds began to spread around Iceland, and early in the 19th century the first were noted breeding on the Faroe Islands.

In 1878 birds nested on Foula, outermost of the Shetland Islands. Since that date there has been a considerable expansion around these islands, and birds now breed inland on abandoned farmlands and on stone walls in some areas. The great cliffs of Hoy in the Orkneys were colonized in 1900 and other islands in the archipelago shortly afterward. Continuing southward, the birds extended down the east coast of Great Britain to Norfolk, where nesting was first noted in 1946. Farther south still, birds continually prospect the Kent coast and will no doubt breed there soon.

In western Britain the story is similar, with birds beginning to nest in Cornwall and Devon in the 1940's following successful colonization farther north. Eastward along the south coast, Fulmars are regularly seen on the Dorset, Isle of Wight and Sussex cliffs, though successful breeding has yet to be confirmed. In Ireland, following an initial colonization in North Mayo in 1911, fulmars have now spread to most suitable cliff areas on all coasts.

Why has this occurred? Although different theories have been put forward, the most probable and generally accepted has been propounded by James Fisher, who has spent a lifetime studying the expansion of this remarkable bird. His hypothesis is that the birds first took advantage of the waste material available during the years of the Greenland whale fishery. As this drew to a close, distant-water fishing commenced, so once again large quantities of offal were available. The fulmar is still spreading, though its rate of increase has slowed down.

North Atlantic Fulmar on land (below) and in flight (opposite)

An example of how a species can extend its range: the rapid increase of the North Atlantic Fulmar around the coast of the British Isles

1897
SHETLAND ISLANDS
1878 1902
1898

1901 1903
1911
ORKNEY ISLANDS

OUTER HEBRIDES 1934 1904 1900
1902 1903 1905
1697 1913 1930 1920
1929 1911
1919 1941 1924 1916
1938
1931
1930 1920
1902 1932
1929 1921
1947
1932 1949
1924 1930
1921
1924 1925 1928
1912 1921 1940 1933
1939
1939
1911 1932 1927
1939 1942 1939
1944 1941 1929
1943 1946 1922
1936

IRELAND
1936 1949
1954 1945
1943
1924 1957
1947
1946 1969 1947
918 1930 1949 1947 1949
913 1949 1955
946 1949 NORFOLK
1938 1969 1950
1940 1957
1944

CORNWALL 1946
1945
1945 1969
1958 1947 1949 ? ISLE OF WIGHT
1949

Fairy Prion (front) and
Broad-billed Prion (rear)

Prions

Prions, or 'whale-birds' as they are often called because of
their frequent feeding associations with these mammals, are
among the smaller members of the family Procellariidae and
belong to the genus *Pachyptila*. This genus contains some six
species and a number of closely related subspecies, all so similar
in size and appearance that they are virtually impossible to
identify when observed at sea. Their general coloration is
blue-gray on the back with white on the underparts and on the
undersurfaces of the wings. The largest species is some 12
inches in length.

All six prions are restricted to the Southern Hemisphere.
The Broad-billed Prion *(Pachyptila vittata)* breeds on Tris-
tan da Cunha, Gough Island and in New Zealand waters.
Salvin's, or the Medium-billed, Prion *(P. salvini)* breeds on
Crozet and Marion Island, while the Fairy Prion *(P. turtur)*,
which on occasion strays north to tropical waters, nests in the
Bass Strait and off New Zealand. The Thin-billed Prion
(P. belcheri) breeds on Kerguelen and on the Falkland
Islands, while the Thick-billed, or Fulmar, Prion *(P. cras-
sirostris)* nests on sub-Antarctic islands south of New
Zealand, Heard and Kerguelen Islands. The last species, the
Dove, or Antarctic, Prion *(P. desolata)*, nests on the Antarc-
tic continent at Cape Denison and islands to the north such
as Kerguelen, Macquarie and Heard.

Detail of prion's bill showing comblike structures, or lamellae, for straining water

At their breeding colonies, prions construct nests in burrows excavated in the peaty soil or in rock crevices. A single white egg is laid which in one of the species studied—the Dove Prion—takes some 45 days to hatch. Chicks are fed by both parents, nightly at first but more erratically toward the end of fledging, which lasts some seven weeks.

Prions feed on zooplankton in the surface layer of the sea. Their bills are adapted for a water-straining procedure by lamellae, comblike structures on either side of the bill that are particularly pronounced in the Broad-billed and Salvin's Prions.

Distribution of six species of prion

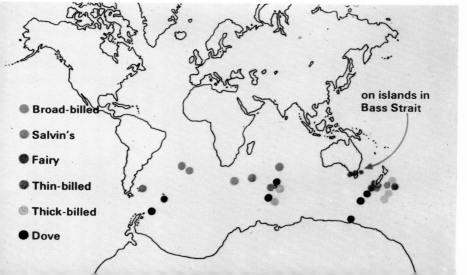

● Broad-billed

● Salvin's

● Fairy

● Thin-billed

● Thick-billed

● Dove

on islands in Bass Strait

Gadfly petrels

Gadfly petrels belong to two genera: *Bulweria,* containing two species, and *Pterodroma,* containing 25. The birds vary in size from between 9 and 10 inches in length to the largest, Schlegel's Petrel *(Pterodroma incerta)* of the South Atlantic, which is some 18 inches long.

Some gadfly petrels, such as the Great-winged Petrel *(P. macroptera),* are widely distributed. This bird breeds on many oceanic islands from Tristan da Cunha eastward to New Zealand and is very numerous in the southern oceans. The Kermadec Petrel *(P. phillipii)* breeds on a scattering of islands from Lord Howe in the Tasman Sea eastward to Juan Fernandez off Chile. It is unusual in that it nests above ground under bushes and shrubs, unlike other species which resort to crevices and burrows. Solander's Petrel breeds only on islands around New Zealand. Others, such as the Reunion Petrel *(P. aterrina),* may be restricted for breeding to a single island or archipelago.

Two of the rarest of gadfly petrels are the Bermuda Petrel, or Cahow *(P. cahow),* and the Black-capped Petrel, or Diablotin *(P. hasitata),* both restricted to the Caribbean region. In 1967 only 22 pairs of the Bermuda Petrel were known to have nested, these on an island off Bermuda, and the future of this species is grim. Besides being preyed upon by White-

Bermuda Petrel, or Cahow, in flight

Great-winged Petrel (left) and Solander's Petrel (right)

tailed Tropic-birds *(Phaeton lepturus)* and rats, against which some protection can be given, the Bermuda Petrels are also threatened by the insidious menace of contamination by D.D.T. This is probably picked up by the birds when they feed on zooplankton which has absorbed the material from contaminated sea water. The birds' breeding success has diminished alarmingly in recent years and the Bermuda Petrel is now threatened with extinction.

Distribution of the Great-winged Petrel, Solander's Petrel and Bermuda Petrel

Great-winged
Solander's
Bermuda

Shearwaters

There are 21 species of shearwater belonging to a number of different genera: *Puffinus*, with 17 species, *Procellaria*, with three, and *Adamastor*, with a single member. All are long-winged and generally have slender bodies. They are so well adapted for a life at sea that they are usually awkward when ashore. In general their color is dark above with white beneath, though some species are completely dark and one is pure white.

Most shearwaters nest in burrows or in crevices, beneath boulders, in ruined walls or even beneath buildings. Colonies may be enormous; that of the Great Shearwater *(Puffinus gravis)* on the 400-acre Nightingale Island in the Tristan da Cunha group may number 3,000,000 birds. A further 300,000 nest on nearby Inaccessible, while on Gough Island a similar number may be found. These are

(Top to bottom)
Audubon's Shearwater,
Greater Shearwater
and Sooty Shearwater

54

Audubon's Shear-
water (left) and Sooty
Shearwater (right) in flight

the only breeding locations for this species, which moves into
the North Atlantic during the southern winter, with large
numbers being seen at times off the western coast of Europe.

Another more widespread species nesting in large numbers
in the Southern Hemisphere is the Sooty Shearwater *(P.
griseus)*. Its main strongholds are the islands and coasts of
New Zealand, with other colonies in southeastern Australian
waters and off the southern tip of South America. Large
numbers move northward in the off-season. In the North
Atlantic the birds congregate in the rich feeding grounds off
the eastern coast of the United States and Canada before
moving across to northern European waters in July and
August, finally returning southward during the autumn
months.

Most shearwaters visit their colonies at night, but not the
Audubon's Shearwater *(P. lherminieri)*; this bird is entirely
diurnal at its colonies in the Galapagos Islands. The colony
on the island of Santa Plaza, off Indefatigable, has been studied
by Dr. M. P. Harris. He discovered that the nests are built
mainly in boulders at the cliff base. The birds appear to nest
throughout the year, but eggs are laid chiefly when good
supplies of food—in this case, zooplankton—are available;
when food is short, egg-laying wanes and may cease altogether.

Manx Shearwaters in flight

Of all the sea birds that breed in European waters, the Manx Shearwater *(P. puffinus)* is probably the one which has received most attention from ornithologists. A bird weighing a little less than two-thirds of a pound, dark gray above and white beneath, it is found only in Bermuda and on certain islands off the west coast of Europe, from Iceland southward to the Azores and Madeira. A subspecies is found in the Mediterranean and another in the Pacific Ocean. Unfortunately, the Manx Shearwater is seldom seen along North American coasts.

One of the largest European colonies is on the island of Skokholm, off South Wales in Britain, where in 1968 a census showed that 35,000 pairs were nesting. Another large colony lives on nearby Skomer, though no census of it has yet been made. These two islands together probably hold the largest concentration of Manx Shearwaters in western Europe.

Manx Shearwater

Nest location (left) and chick of Manx Shearwater (right)

The Skokholm colony has been studied by R. M. Lockley, who moved there in 1927; in the years that followed much interesting work was done on the shearwater colony close to his farmhouse. His work was interrupted by the war but is admirably portrayed in his book, *Shearwaters*. Since 1946 further studies have been carried out. Large numbers of birds have been banded, either chicks at the nest or adults caught at night by hand with the aid of a flashlight.

From the banding recoveries we have learned that many young birds go south to Brazilian waters within a few weeks after leaving the nesting burrow. One bird wandered, or was windblown, across the southern oceans to be recovered in Australia. From all the evidence available so far it would seem that Manx Shearwaters are very long-lived birds and probably do not breed until they are five years old.

Breeding range and migration route of the Manx Shearwater

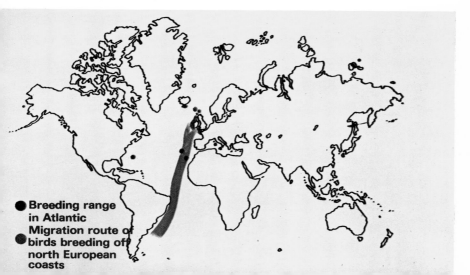

Short-tailed Shearwater

A single white egg is laid in late April or early May and takes 52 days to hatch. The chicks remain in the burrow for ten weeks before leaving for the sea, by this time deserted by their parents. It is during this period that many chicks are lost through both disease and predation, for they fall easy prey to marauding Great Black-backed Gulls *(Larus marinus)*, as the numerous carcasses around the colonies bear silent witness.

The Short-tailed Shearwater *(P. tenuirostris)* breeds on islands off Victoria, South Australia, Tasmania and in the Bass Strait, where it forms large colonies. Some colonies, even on small islands, are thought to contain as many as 250,000 pairs, while the total population must measure millions of birds, making this species one of the most numerous sea birds in the world.

Similar to the Sooty Shearwater, which breeds in smaller numbers in the same area and forms much larger colonies elsewhere (see pages 54 to 55), the Short-tailed can be distinguished from it in the field by its smaller size and paler underwing.

Birds begin to return to their colonies during October, but it is not until the latter half of November that the eggs are laid. A single, large white egg is laid which, if lost, is not replaced during the season, a procedure found throughout the shearwater family. Incubation, which is shared by both parents, takes between 53 and 57 days. The chick, covered with down at first, grows rapidly on the rich, though erratic, meals it receives. When it is about 12 weeks old, the parents cease feeding it. The chicks remain in their burrows, fasting for up to two weeks before they leave for the sea and begin to fend for themselves.

After leaving the breeding colonies, the birds head north-west across the Pacific toward Japanese waters, making use of prevailing winds; then, still using favorable winds, they cross toward Alaska and then south toward the United States. Then they swing away from land again on a southwesterly course which eventually returns them to the breeding area. This vast 20,000-mile journey is made during the off-season, and tremendous distances are covered in quite short periods; for example, one bird reached Japan, 5,500 miles from its Tasmanian colony, within a month.

A local name in Australia and New Zealand is the 'Mutton-bird', and the Short-tailed Shearwater figures prominently in the economy of some islands. Large numbers of well-grown young are taken under license each season. After the stomach oil has been removed — for use in drugs and cosmetics — and the down plucked for sleeping bags, the birds are packed in brine barrels or canned and sold as 'Tasmanian Squab'. When cooked, they have a pleasant taste.

Migration routes of the Short-tailed Shearwater

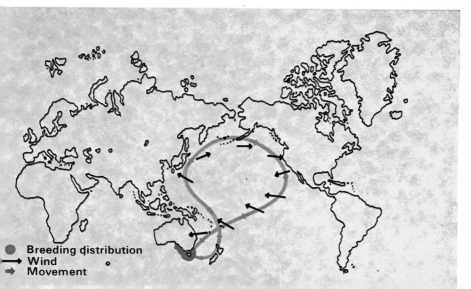

● **Breeding distribution**
➡ **Wind**
➡ **Movement**

Diving petrels

The diving petrels of the family Pelecanoididae contain four species in one genus, *Pelecanoides*, and belong to the large order of Procellariiformes, which also contains the shearwaters and petrels. They are, however, very different in appearance from the other members of this order; with their stubby bodies, short necks and wings they closely resemble the Little Auk, or Dovekie *(Plautus alle)*, of Arctic seas, a similarity first noted by Charles Darwin during the voyage of the *Beagle*.

All four species are small; the largest, the Peruvian Diving Petrel *(P. garnotii)*, does not exceed 10 inches in length though it has double the bulk of the others. Three are very similar in appearance, with glossy black plumage above and white beneath and are very difficult, if not impossible, to differentiate at sea. The other, the Magellan Diving Petrel *(P. magellani)* has distinctive white-tipped feathers on its back and wings, while two white neck patches almost form a collar. In all four species the bill is black, while the legs and feet are of various shades, sometimes very bright blue, as in the Georgian Diving Petrel *(P. georgicus)*.

Diving petrels are restricted to the Southern Hemisphere between latitudes 35 degrees and 60 degrees except for the Peruvian species, which extends northward in the cool conditions of the Humboldt Current to Peru. Although they may be encountered at sea, often at a considerable distance from

Breeding ranges of the four species of diving petrels

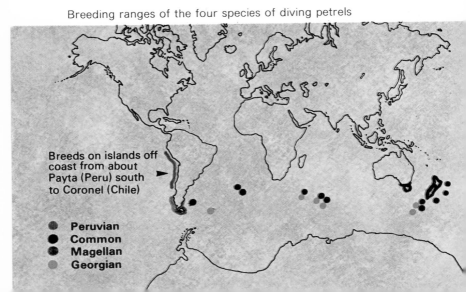

Breeds on islands off coast from about Payta (Peru) south to Coronel (Chile) ➤

● Peruvian
● Common
◐ Magellan
● Georgian

Peruvian Diving Petrel (top) and
Common Diving Petrel (bottom)

land, most are sedentary and stay in the vicinity of their breeding colonies. These are generally situated on rocky islands, though the birds may travel several miles inland and climb to a considerable height in order to obtain a suitable nest site. The site may be in a hollow beneath rocks or a burrow excavated by the birds themselves in soft soil. The Peruvian species formerly nested in vast numbers in the deep guano beds on the islands off the coasts of Chile and Peru, but now that much of the guano has been removed, this species has greatly diminished. Diving petrels lay a single white egg. Both parents take turns in the incubation, which lasts for about eight weeks in the Common Diving Petrel *(P. urinatrix)*, so far the only species studied in detail. The chick is fed on partially digested fish and crustaceans for 7 weeks before it leaves for the sea. Unlike many other Procellariiformes, diving petrels mature at an early age and breed when only two years old.

61

Georgian Diving
Petrel in flight

As we have seen, the diving petrels resemble the Little Auk
in superficial respects. This latter species belongs to the
Alcidae, or auks, a family widely separated from the Procellariiformes and one which has no representatives in the Southern Hemisphere. The ecological niche used in the north by the
Alcidae is filled in their absence by the diving petrels of the
south. Although looking quite unlike other members of the
Procellariiformes, the diving petrels do retain a number of
typical characteristics such as nasal tubes and bill plates, the
nostrils opening upward side by side at the base of the bill.
At the same time their size, shape, basic coloration, body
weight, mode of flight and skeletal features resemble those of
the Little Auk.

Diving petrels inhabit coastal waters, rather than roaming
the oceans as do other shearwaters and petrels. Because of this,
long wings and slender bodies, so necessary for sustained
gliding day after day at sea, are not required and have given
way to short wings and a rapid whirring flight. Like auks,
groups of diving petrels may be observed flying in straight
lines low across the sea or having difficulty in taking off from
the surface during calm weather. Living a coastal existence
enables them to visit their nest sites much more frequently, and

there is no need for the long periods of fasting during incubation which are undergone by many shearwaters and petrels. For the same reason, the chicks may be brooded longer and fed more regularly.

Instead of finding their food on the surface of the sea or just beneath it, the diving petrels, as their name suggests, actively search for their food—crustaceans and small fish such as anchovies—beneath the waves. Like the Little Auk, they will dive straight into the sea directly from flight, briefly holding their wings motionless prior to entering the water. Once beneath the surface, both wings and feet are used for propulsion. The birds remain submerged for only a short period before breaking the surface and resuming their flight without a pause, often flying only a short distance before diving to feed again.

Some, if not all, of the diving petrels become flightless for a time during molting, though this does not seem to impair their agility in catching underwater prey. It is believed that the ability to use their wings beneath the surface at the same time they are temporarily unable to fly is an evolutionary stage which penguins must have passed through before becoming completely flightless.

Magellan Diving
Petrel chasing a fish

Tropic- or bo's'n-birds

The three species of tropic-birds — they are sometimes called bo's'n-birds because of their high shrilling notes, which resemble those given on the boatswain's pipe — are found in tropical or subtropical seas.

The largest is the Red-tailed Tropic-bird *(Phaëthon rubricauda)*, found in the tropical Indian and Pacific Oceans where it occurs in a number of subspecies. Its length, not including the central tail feathers, may reach 18 inches, while the smaller Red-billed Tropic-bird *(P. aeth'ereus)* reaches 14 inches. This species lives in the Galapagos Islands, along the west coast of Central America, the Caribbean, tropical Atlantic, Red Sea and Persian Gulf coasts. Smallest of all,

White-tailed Tropic-bird

only 12 inches or so in length, is the White-tailed Tropic-bird *(P. lepturus)*, sometimes known as the Yellow-billed. It ranges from the Caribbean eastward through the Atlantic and Indian Oceans to the southwestern Pacific.

Although tropic-birds are similar to gulls and terns in some respects, their flight is rapid with quick wingbeats like that of a pigeon, quite unlike any other sea bird. Food in the form of fish and squid is caught by diving just below the surface from heights of up to 50 feet.

All three species are ungainly on land because their short legs are set far back, and they therefore choose nest sites with

Red-tailed Tropic-bird

easy access to the sea. A single brownish egg is laid in a bare
scrape beneath rocks or vegetation. Depending on the species,
the egg takes between 41 and 45 days to hatch. The chicks,
which at first are covered with grayish down, grow slowly
and remain in the nest for up to 15 weeks before fledging.

Recent studies at breeding grounds have shown that a
complete cycle takes from 9 to 12 months on Ascension
Island and 10 months on the Galapagos. Because the breeding season is a disturbed affair, with many egg and chick
losses, it may be spread throughout the year, though with
distinct peaks of egg-laying at certain times.

Red-billed Tropic-bird and Red-tailed Tropic-bird in flight

Frigate- or 'man-o'-war' birds

Frigate-birds are probably the most aerial of all sea birds, vying with land birds such as the swifts for being the most aerial of all birds. With their long wings they soar for hours almost without effort, seldom settling on the water. They are not adapted for life on the surface, as their feet are small and have reduced webs, while their oil glands are not sufficient to prevent their plumage from quickly becoming saturated.

There are five species of frigate-birds, while the precise number of subspecies — 14 are usually listed — is still a question for debate. They are found throughout the tropical and subtropical oceans of the world, though they remain close to the vicinity of their breeding colonies. Although on occasion one may be sighted at some distance out to sea, usually the presence of frigate-birds is a sure indicator that land is close at hand.

The largest of all, the Magnificent Frigate-bird *(Fregata magnificens),* has a wingspread of up to 8 feet and has the biggest wingspread in proportion to body weight of any bird. Although their range is restricted to subtropical American waters with an offshoot at Cape Verde, one was caught in a landing net on a small freshwater lake in Scotland in July 1953. This is the first record of this species in the British Isles, though there are a number of other North Atlantic sightings.

Distribution of the five species of frigate-birds

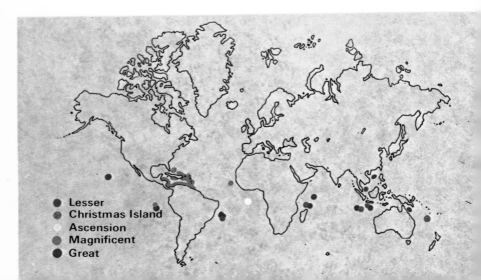

● Lesser
● Christmas Island
○ Ascension
● Magnificent
● Great

Male Magnificent Frigate-bird with gular pouch inflated

The Great *(F. minor)* and Lesser Frigate-birds *(F. ariel)* are both widespread species, while the Ascension Frigate-bird *(F. aquila)* is found only on Boatswain Island in the Ascension group. The last species, the Christmas Island Frigate-bird *(F. andrewsi)*, is restricted to Christmas Island and several other remote sites in the eastern Indian Ocean.

The islanders on some archipelagos in the central Pacific Ocean have taken advantage of the birds' apparent tameness and trained them to carry messages from island to island. Birds are trained by feeding to use perches close to buildings, and messages are carried in reed tubes attached to the wings.

Living in the tropical zone enables the birds to breed all the year round, though variations in food supply, which are probably related to weather changes, seem to ensure a definite nesting cycle.

During the courtship sessions the male develops a large, crimson gular sac, or throat pouch, which is inflated during display. When fully extended, it obscures the whole front of the bird except for the top of the head and the eyes, which just peer over. The males take up a suitable site and sit, often for hours on end, with pouch inflated, while the larger females fly overhead. As a prospective mate passes nearby, the wings are spread and there is much bill rattling and harsh cackling.

Breeding colonies of frigate-birds are usually on small, undisturbed islands. The nests are large, untidy structures of sticks placed in anything from a low bush to a mangrove tree 60 feet high. In the absence of suitable vegetation, birds may nest on the ground. The single, large

(Top to bottom) Lesser Frigate-bird, Great Frigate-bird, female Ascension Frigate-bird, Christmas Island Frigate-bird

Male Ascension Frigate-birds in flight

white egg is incubated by both parents and hatches at between 40 and 50 days. At first the chick is naked, and is closely
brooded until about 2 weeks old, when a growth of down
begins to afford protection. Chicks are fed on fish and scraps
regurgitated by the parents; the exact period of the young
birds' dependence is not known. They are fully fledged after
four or five months. For a considerable time after this (it may
be for as long as six months) the chicks are fed by the
parents, at the same time gradually learning through scavenging about the colony how to fend for themselves.

Colonies are often situated close to those of other sea birds,
which provide a source of food. The frigate-bird acts in an
aggressive and piratical manner (from which it no doubt de-
rives its names), chasing other species and forcing them to
drop or disgorge their food, which is then caught adeptly and
swallowed in mid-air. Another method of obtaining food is by
swooping low over a tern colony and snatching up unguarded
eggs or chicks. Frigate-birds are able to hunt for themselves and
easily seize flying fish in the air as they emerge from the waves.
Refuse floating on the surface of the sea is eagerly sought,
while newly hatched turtles making their way down a beach
provide an easy meal.

Cormorants and shags

This is a family of large sea birds with representatives in most parts of the world, including many of the great river systems of Africa and Asia. The family Phalacrocoracidae has three genera: *Phalacrocorax* with 24 species, *Haliëtor* with four and *Nannopterum* with a single species.

Two species occur in the British Isles. The Great Cormorant *(P. carbo)*, known in some places as the Common Cormorant, is a very widely distributed species. The other is the Shag *(P. aristotelis)*, or Green Cormorant. This name is also used as an alternative for several Southern Hemisphere species.

Cormorants range in size from the Pigmy Cormorant *(H. pygmeus)*, some 19 inches in length, to the Great Cormorant of about 40 inches. Cormorants are generally black or dark colored, though some species have white underparts. They are sociable birds and gather in large colonies to nest, while nonbreeding or off-duty birds often collect on favorite rocks or cliffs. Nests are usually bulky structures, and several eggs are laid.

The birds are all expert divers, diving from the surface of the water by means of a distinct forward leap. Wings are generally not used under the surface, since the large webbed feet are efficient propulsion units which drive the birds to a considerable depth when necessary. There are reports of fishermen having caught marine species in their nets at depths of 70

Distribution of Great Cormorant

and even 100 feet. It is thought that hearing plays an important part in the underwater search for food, a search that often brings them into conflict with fishermen.

The Guanay Cormorant *(P. bougainvillei)* has been described as the most valuable wild bird in the world. It nests in huge colonies on islands off the coast of Chile and Peru. Vast numbers of these birds, their ranks swelled by other species like the Peruvian Booby *(Sula variegata),* feed in the plankton-rich waters of the Humboldt Current and use predator-free islands for nesting. Vast quantities of droppings, or guano, have accumulated over thousands of years, since little rain falls to wash the material away. A single Guanay Cormorant with a voracious appetite for anchovies deposits more than 2 pounds of guano a month.

It was not until about 1840 that men began to seriously exploit these deposits for fertilizer, though previously they had been used by the Incas and other local peoples. Once governments became interested, the deposits were stripped with no thought as to their replenishment, and species like the Peruvian Diving Petrel and Peruvian Penguin, both important guano producers, began to vanish as their nest sites were destroyed. Between 1848 and 1875 more than 20 million tons worth nearly 172 billion dollars were exported. With stocks rapidly diminishing, action was urgently required, and in 1909 a system of annual 'cropping' was instigated.

The colonies are again flourishing, and new ones have also been established on predator-free headlands on the mainland. The main danger now seems to be that man's overfishing of the area will reduce the colonies, which must surely rank as one of the seven wonders of the avian world.

There are other guano islands off southwestern Africa. In this area the important species are the Cape Cormorant *(P. capensis)*, the Cape Gannet *(Sula capensis)* and the Jackass Penguin. There, too, after a period of careless overexploitation the guano industry is on a balanced 'cropping' basis.

Locations of guano-producing areas

Cape Cormorant (left) and
Guanay Cormorant (right)

In Asia, man has also utilized cormorants, though for a completely different purpose — catching fish. Two species, the Great Cormorant and the Japanese Cormorant *(P. capillatus)*, have been used in many countries, including Japan, China and India. The latter species is usually caught by using bird-lime and decoys on the rocks which the cormorants have used for roosting during the winter months. In other instances the birds may be specially bred for the purpose and sold, normally untrained, to fishermen. The colonies from which the birds are taken receive special protection, and there are instances of this going back over hundreds of years.

The cormorants are trained to fish with a leather collar around their necks. The collar prevents them from swallowing the catch and is also a convenient place to attach the line by which they are held. Training may take only a few weeks before the birds become proficient.

In Japan the art dates back to at least the sixth century A.D. and there are records of the catches sent to the Emperor dating back to 900 A.D. Fishing takes place on the Nagono River, where certain sections have been set aside for this purpose. The season is from May 11 to October 15, and fishing is conducted every night except when there is a full moon. Now the custom is a major tourist attraction, rather than a means of providing food.

Japanese fishermen using cormorants to catch fish for them

The fishing is carried out after dark from boats, each carrying a large flare at the stern which attracts the fish to the vicinity. Each boat has a crew of four, one of whom is known as the Usho, or Cormorant Master, and has 12 birds in his charge. Another, known as *Uzukai*, has control of four birds, the other members having responsibility for the boat and for the flare. The birds are removed from their baskets in a certain order, beginning with the youngest. Once in the water the birds quickly start to hunt the fish lured to the area. The birds swallow the fish as far as the collar and are then gently pulled back on board and the catch removed. If fish are plentiful, as many as 50 may be caught by a well-trained bird in one night.

In China the art seems to date from at least the Sung dynasty (960–1298 A.D.), when fishing was carried out by day from rafts moored on the rivers. Birds were often bred in captivity rather than taken wild from colonies. With the advent of modern fishing methods, the old custom began dying out.

The method flourished briefly as a sport in Great Britain under the Stuart kings, and the post of Master of the Cormorants was created. The birds were kept on ponds near the present site of the Houses of Parliament.

One species of cormorant is unique: the large Flightless Cormorant *(Nannopterum harrisi)* of the Galapagos Islands. It is about 3 feet in length and its brownish plumage, with paler underparts, is short and dense like that of a penguin. The wings are much reduced in size, the flight feathers in particular being reduced in number as well as size. In fact, its wings are smaller in comparison with overall size than those of the extinct Great Auk (see pages 136 to 137). It is an expert swimmer, though when diving only the powerful webbed feet are used for propulsion, the wings remaining folded.

Because the Flightless Cormorant lives in an isolated area, with an adequate all-year-round food supply and no natural predators, it is an excellent example of a bird that has lost the power of flight when it was no longer required. Even within the Galapagos Islands the bird's range is restricted to Albermarle and Narborough, while most are concentrated in the shallow strait between the two islands. The population is small. In 1961 it was considered to be about 500 pairs, a fact which causes some concern, though at the present time the numbers show no sign of a decline.

Birds breed in all months of the year, but the peak time is from April to June, a period when the Humboldt Current extends northward and influences the food supply favorably. Prior to and during nest building there is much display from both sexes, usually taking the form of water dances. The birds swim about and, as they pass each other, bend their necks into an 'S' curve. At a later stage, the male will lead the female ashore to a prospective nest site, often encouraging her with low growls. Nests are bulky, constructed from seaweed torn from the rocks. The male collects the material while the female remains on guard and carries out the construction.

Three eggs are the usual clutch, and both parents take part in the incubation, the precise period of which is as yet unknown. Usually only a single youngster is reared, as some eggs fail to hatch and many small chicks die. One parent always remains on guard at the nest site with the chick, which is fed on fish and octopus. The fledging period is not known, but after leaving the nest, chicks are fed for a while at sea.

Flightless Cormorant of the Galapagos Islands

Several species of cormorant are found in the Antarctic and sub-Antarctic regions. They are often called shags in their breeding areas, perhaps from the long, shaggy plumes which several species grow—and quickly shed—during the breeding season. In Britain this name is restricted to the bird known elsewhere as the Green Cormorant, to distinguish it from the Great Cormorant, the only other native species.

The Magellan Cormorant *(P. magellanicus)* is found, as its name suggests, in the Straits of Magellan and on the islands around Cape Horn. It extends northward along the southern coasts of Patagonia and Chile and also lives in the Falkland Islands. This species may be distinguished from the similar Blue-eyed Cormorant *(P. atriceps)* by its red face and feathered throat, while in the breeding season it has a white neck. Some authorities consider that the Magellan Cormorant is just a subspecies of the Blue-eyed. The latter breeds in much the same area, though it extends farther north by several hundred miles. It also nests well to the south on islands off Grahamland, in South Georgia, the South Orkneys and Shetlands and in the South Sandwich group.

The King Cormorant *(P. albiventer)* is similar in size and appearance to the Blue-eyed, from which it can be distinguished by the extensions of purple-black plumage from the bill area and the absence of a white back patch. This species also breeds on the coasts of Patagonia and in the Falkland Islands, while farther east it occurs in two subspecies on Crozet Island and Macquarie Island.

Blue-eyed Cormorant

Double-crested
Cormorant (left),
Kerguelen Cormorant
(center) and King
Cormorant (right)

The Kerguelen Cormorant *(P. verrucosus)* is found nesting only on Kerguelen Island. On South Island in New Zealand and on the sub-Antarctic islands farther south, the Rough-legged Cormorant *(P. carunculatus)* occurs, together with some five subspecies, or perhaps only insular races, which can be recognized by the color of the face and caruncles at the base of the bill.

Several species of cormorant live in the great river systems of the world, rather than on the sea coasts, while others, such as the Double-crested Cormorant *(P. auritus)*, frequent both habitats and may be seen on coasts, rivers and inland lakes. This species is very common all around North America.

Reed Cormorant

All four species in the genus *Haliëtor* appear on inland waters, along with the Indian Cormorant *(P. fuscicollis)*, which is also found in Ceylon and Burma, and the Little Black Cormorant *(P. sulcirostris)* of the Malay archipelago and Australasia.

The Pigmy Cormorant is rarely seen on the coast. Its range extends from southeastern Europe eastward through Turkey and Iran as far as Afghanistan. Breeding colonies of this shy species may be quite large and are found among low bushes or in reedbeds. They will often include other species, such as herons and egrets. The Pigmy Cormorant is a handsome species with glossy green plumage heavily spotted with white, while in summer its head is a dark red-brown. Although rather clumsy on land, the birds are dextrous as they clamber about the vegetation. They frequently perch on a vertical stem by sitting, literally 'on their tails', pressing them hard against the stem for support.

The Reed Cormorant, or Long-tailed Shag *(H. africanus)*, is found northward from the Cape of Good Hope to Gambia and the Sudan, with a subspecies on Madagascar. A bird of solitary habits, it swims lower in the water than other species.

The Javanese, or Little, Cormorant *(H. niger)* is found throughout India, Burma, Ceylon, the Malay Peninsula, Borneo and nearby islands. It may be distinguished from the Indian Cormorant by its smaller size, short bill and relatively long tail.

The Little Pied Cormorant *(H. melanoleucus)* inhabits many of the Indonesian islands, New Guinea, Australia, Tasmania, New Zealand and New Caledonia. Subspecies have been described in a number of these areas. Except for the New Zealand race, the underparts are white, and birds can be distinguished from other white-breasted species by their short bill and neck and long tail.

The Shag, or Green Cormorant, nests along rocky coasts from the White Sea and Iceland southward to Morocco. It is also at home in the Mediterranean and Aegean Seas and on the Crimean coast of the Black Sea. Strictly a bird of open coastlines, the Shag rarely enters far into estuaries and comes inland only when driven by storms. When diving for food, it stays below for about a minute, though occasional dives of longer

Pigmy Cormorant (left) and Indian Cormorant (right)

Adult Shag and chick

duration have been recorded. It is interesting to note the difference in the fish taken by the Shag and the Great Cormorant. The former takes a large proportion of sand eels while the latter takes a great quantity of flat fish; indeed, half of its diet is said to be of marketable value.

With glossy green plumage, only offset by the yellow mouthparts, the Shag is a very handsome bird. Early in the breeding season its head is adorned with a forward-curving crest, though this quickly disappears as the season proceeds. Colonies of this species may be large, like those of other cormorants, but in many instances pairs nest individually or in small groups. Typical sites are among boulders, on cliff ledges and in the dark recesses of sea caves.

Their nests are large, bulky structures made from nearby seaweed and vegetation. Any suitable piece of flotsam may also be added; a child's plastic tractor was found on one occasion. The normal clutch is three eggs, though up to six have been recorded. Incubation, which is carried out by both parents, is not by the conventional brood-patch, for this is absent in the cormorants. Instead, the heat of the large webbed feet is used, the bird shuffling them beneath the eggs when settling on the nest. The incubation period is from 30 to 34 days; the chicks are jet-black, blind, naked and helpless when they hatch.

Chicks are fed on regurgitated fish and soon become covered in brownish down. This is finally replaced by brown feathers which are paler underneath. Fledging takes place during the seventh week, though some chicks are looked after by their parents for up to an additional seven weeks. During this time the birds collect in large numbers on favorite rocks. Later, when dispersal takes place, some individuals roam several hundred miles from the colony, though adults seem more sedentary.

The Shag has been increasing in numbers in Great Britain during recent years, particularly in northeastern England and southeastern Scotland. Although changes in the available food supply have been suggested as the reason for this, it seems more likely to be due to the cessation of human persecution.

(Top to bottom) Young Shags in second winter and summer, first winter and summer, and juvenile plumage

Distribution of North Atlantic Gannet

Gannets

The headquarters of the North Atlantic Gannet *(Morus bassanus)* are the colonies around Great Britain and Ireland, the largest being those on the great stacks of St. Kilda where gannets have nested for 1,000 years or more; 44,529 pairs nested in 1959. A colony on Lundy Island in the Bristol Channel became extinct during the 19th century, at the same time as one was becoming established on Grassholme off the south-

North Atlantic Gannet

North Atlantic Gannet diving and in flight

western coast of Wales. In 1964 this colony contained 15,528 pairs.

Elsewhere in the North Atlantic, colonies have been founded in recent years in Norway, the Channel Islands and off Brittany. Others, sometimes large, whose early history is often obscure, are located in the Faroes, Newfoundland, Iceland and Canada. The North Atlantic Gannet has nested on Bird Rock and Bonaventure Island in the Gulf of St. Lawrence.

Measuring some 3 feet in length, the North Atlantic Gannet is the largest bird to frequent the coastal waters of the North Atlantic, ranging in winter from North Carolina south to the Gulf of Mexico. European populations of these birds move southward to North Africa and the Canary Islands. They can be seen in small flocks at almost any time of the year, fishing just beyond the breakers. To catch its prey, the North Atlantic Gannet circles at a height of 60 to 100 feet above the water, then, seeing a fish, dives headlong with folded wings into the water. The speed of impact when the bird enters the water is often great enough to send a sea spray several feet into the air. In a few seconds it reappears with its prey, which is swallowed whole. The fish taken by this method are often large, and gannets can greatly distend their throats to accomodate them.

As we have seen in the preceding pages, gannets resort to large, densely packed colonies for breeding. Each nest is placed just beyond the reach of its neighbors, but no farther. It is generally a bulky structure made from seaweed and grass which may be as much as 2 feet high, with sloping sides and a hollow for the egg. Such nests are necessary to keep the egg or chick out of the guano slime which forms the nest site of the colony.

A single egg is laid, usually during April. Like the cormorants, the gannets have no brood-patch and they carry out incubation by placing their webbed feet, slightly over-lapping, on the egg. The egg takes 42 days to hatch and both sexes share the incubation. The chick takes about 36 hours to emerge from the time the chipping commences. During this time the egg rests on the upper surface of the parent's feet.

Weighing about 2 ounces when hatched, the chick will increase to a maximum weight of about 10 pounds by the time it is nine weeks old. During the first two weeks, chicks are brooded by one or other parent, and even after this period one will remain on guard while the other is away fishing. Food is brought back in the throat of the adult, from which it is removed by the chick forcing its own bill deep inside. The first growth of down is white, but this is eventually replaced by mottled brown feathers; adult plumage is not attained until the fourth

Breeding areas and movements of North Atlantic Gannets

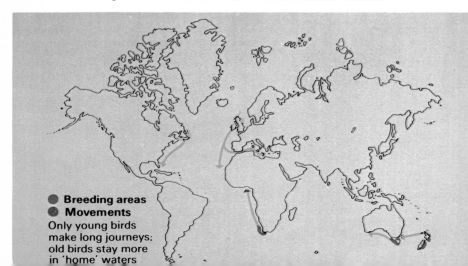

● **Breeding areas**
● **Movements**
**Only young birds
make long journeys;
old birds stay more
in 'home' waters**

Sweeping bows to one another

Aggression between two adults

Chick 'bill hiding' at the approach of an adult

Friendly ceremony performed when birds meet at nesting site

Chick pestering adult

Adult feeding chick

Display postures of North Atlantic Gannets

year of life, when the young birds begin to breed.

Chicks that are on the edge of a colony leave the nest in comparative comfort, but others may have to stagger many yards, set about on all sides by angry adults whose nests they pass. If conditions are right, the first flight may last for several miles. The chick is now alone, though with ample fat reserves it can survive without food for up to three weeks. During this time it must learn to fish and fly, a stage of its life which may never be fully observed by man.

Young gannets are great wanderers. In the first years of life many go south to spend their time off the coasts of West Africa. Later they will remain more in home waters, deserting the colonies only during the brief midwinter months.

Two other species of gannet, the Cape Gannet, or Malgash *(M. capensis),* and the Australian Gannel *(M. serrator),* are found in the Southern Hemisphere, but differences from the northern species are slight.

The Cape Gannet nests on a scattering of islands off South Africa, where all the colonies are strictly protected. Aerial means have been used to effect accurate surveys of the population, which is estimated to be about 500,000 pairs. Unlike most North Atlantic colonies, those of the Cape Gannet tend to be on fairly flat, low islands. The eggs are laid in October and the incubation and fledging periods are similar to those of the northern species.

Large numbers of Cape Gannet chicks have been banded, and again it has been found that it is the juveniles which wander most. Many move north to the Gulf of Guinea in the first months of life, though later they return to home waters and become more sedentary.

The Cape Gannet, along with the Cape Cormorant and Jackass Penguin, is an important guano producer. It is said that gannets nesting on the same islands as the penguins leave passages through their colonies in order to give the penguins easy access to and from the sea.

Cape Gannet

Distribution of Cape and Australian Gannets

The Australian Gannet breeds on islands in the Bass Strait and off Tasmania, while others are found off North Island, New Zealand. It has a much smaller population than its relatives, in the early 1950's being estimated at about 21,000 pairs. Again banding studies have shown that most movement takes place during the first years of life, with New Zealand birds traveling eastward to Australian waters.

Australian Gannet

Boobies

The six species of booby are found throughout the warm oceans of the world. Included in the same family as the gannets, they are similar to them in many respects. For example, they use the same plunge-diving mode of catching prey, though with adaptations. The Brown Booby *(Sula leucogaster)* makes more shallow, angled dives while the Red-footed Booby *(S. sula)* will take flying fish as well as squid, which it catches on the surface at night.

The Red-footed Booby is found on many islands in the Caribbean, South Atlantic, Indian and Pacific Oceans, including the Galapagos Islands, where an enormous colony of some 140,000 pairs nests on Tower Island. It is one of two booby species which nest in trees and bushes, sometimes at a con-

Brown Booby (top) and
Blue-faced Booby (bottom)

siderable height above the ground. The single egg takes about 46 days to hatch. The chick, like those of other members of the family, is quite helpless at first and is brooded by one or other parent until it is about six weeks old. The fledging period varies somewhat between different breeding sites, ranging from 14 to 19 weeks. Though able to fly, the chicks continue to return to their nest sites to be fed for as long as an additional 15 weeks.

The Brown Booby is also found in the Caribbean, tropical Atlantic and Indian Oceans. At Ascension Island, where it has received particular attention, pairs stay at the nest site throughout the year and can therefore commence breeding very quickly when the food supply reaches an adequate level. If food becomes scarce, growing chicks can fast for a considerable period, their growth slowing or stopping entirely.

The Blue-faced Booby (*S. dactylatra*) is a regular summer visitor to Florida, though it breeds on South Atlantic and South Pacific islands.

Red-footed Booby

The Blue-footed Booby *(S. nebouxii)* is the largest species, being some 34 inches in length. It nests on a scattering of islands from Mexico south to Ecuador and Peru, and its two, occasionally three, eggs take about 41 days to hatch. Chicks fledge by about the 14th week and are cared for by their parents for an additional seven weeks. The birds are at least partially nocturnal and may bring food into the colony during the hours of darkness, though whether it is actually caught at night is not known.

Abbot's Booby nests only on Christmas Island in the Indian Ocean, often in trees and bushes; the most recent estimate of its population is 2,000 pairs.

The Peruvian Booby *(S. variegata)*, or 'piquero', breeds only on islands off Peru, where it forms vast colonies, one of which was estimated in 1964 to contain 356,340 pairs; the total population must run into many millions. This is a species which, along with the Guanay Cormorant, is a most efficient guano producer. In fact, its nest is no more than a bowl of droppings into which a few feathers are incorporated as they fall, along with an occasional piece of seaweed.

The clutch consists of three, sometimes four, eggs which take about 43 days to hatch. The chicks are guarded throughout

Peruvian Booby

Distribution of Blue-footed, Peruvian and Abbot's Boobies

● Blue-footed
● Peruvian
● Abbott's

the fledging period by one or the other parent, unlike the other boobies, who leave their chicks for a while in order to search for food. The fledging period is thought to be about 14 weeks, though the chicks are not independent for some time after this.

Blue-footed Booby (front) and
Abbot's Booby (rear)

From time to time the vast sea bird colonies off Peru suffer catastrophic declines in numbers. The cool, food-rich currents are pushed back south by warmer waters from the north — the El Nino. This quickly affects the food supply and hundreds of thousands of birds die, chicks starve to death and eggs lie unincubated. However, once the current systems revert to normal, the superabundant food supply is reestablished and the colonies recoup their losses at an almost staggering rate.

Pelicans

Pelicans belong to a single genus; opinions differ among ornithologists as to whether there are six, seven or eight species, due to the number of subspecies which have been described. They are found in many parts of the world, mainly in tropical regions but also in more temperate zones. Some species prefer estuaries, rivers and inland lakes, while others are strictly oceanic in their habits. The range of some species is discontinuous. For instance, the Eastern White Pelican (*Pelecanus onocrotalus*) inhabits a number of lakes and rivers in southeastern Europe, the Middle East, Asiatic Russia and Africa south to the Cape of Good Hope. Many hundreds of miles may separate one breeding area from another.

They are all large birds, the Dalmatian Pelican (*P. crispus*) being 6 feet in length, while the Brown Pelican (*P. occidentalis*), the smallest, is some 4 feet. These pelicans are well known because they are often kept in zoos and frequently appear in cartoons and advertisements. The long beak, complete with large extendible gular pouch, is of special interest. It is used as a net for catching fish which are promptly swallowed; it is not a storage organ, despite its reputed ability to hold 'enough food for a week'!

Although pelicans seem ungainly on land and their take-off from water is a laborious affair, once airborne they are magnificent. Flying in long lines with necks retracted, they may achieve quite a high altitude under favorable circumstances.

(Top to bottom) Dalmatian Pelican, Australian Pelican and American White Pelican

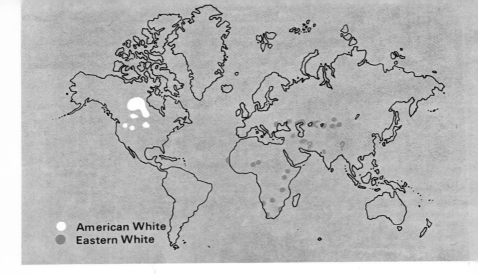

American White
Eastern White

Distribution of American White and Eastern White Pelicans

Several species are migratory, at least in parts of their range. The American White Pelican *(P. erythrorhynchos)* nests from western Canada south to the central and western United States. Its autumn migration takes it southeast to the Gulf of Mexico and the Caribbean area. The Eastern White Pelican leaves the north of its breeding area in winter and moves south to the Persian Gulf, India and the Malay Peninsula.

Pelicans are often communal in their feeding. Birds will form into lines in order to drive fish in toward shallow water by beating their wings on the surface. The Brown Pelican dives for food like the gannets; while doing so it keeps its neck retracted as during flight. The food requirements of such large birds are prodigious. An Eastern White Pelican is thought to eat 10 percent of its body weight in fish per day, (i.e., between 30 and 40 ounces). If this is the case, the colony at Lake Rukwa with 40,000 pairs, the largest in Africa, would consume 17,000 tons of fish in a year.

Pelican colonies are usually large, noisy and smelly avian metropolises. Nests are bulky affairs of sticks placed in bushes and trees, as in the case of the African Pink-backed Pelican *(P. rufescens)*, or on the ground, often among reeds, as in the American White Pelican.

Southeastern Asia has one species of pelican, the Gray

Pelican *(P. philippensis),* and the Australian Pelican *(P. conspicillatus)* inhabits the Australo-Papuan region.

Up to four eggs are laid, usually pale blue in color. Both parents take turns with the incubation, the period of which depends on the species and varies between 30 and 40 days. Chicks are helpless and naked at first and are brooded continuously when first hatched. Later the parents just stand over them to afford some shade from the sun. The chicks are fed on partially digested fish, which they obtain by thrusting their own head deep into the parent's throat.

Among ground-nesting pelicans, the first four weeks or so in a chick's life are spent in the nest area, after which they form into groups or 'pods'. Even when these groups are very large, chicks are fed by their own parents and will seek them out in order to receive a meal. Fledging is accomplished at about the tenth week.

Gray Pelican (top) and
Pink-backed Pelican (bottom)

The Brown Pelican is a bird of the Western Hemisphere, occurring in a number of subspecies from California and South Carolina southward through the Caribbean zone to South America. On the east coast it does not extend farther south than the delta of the Orinoco. In the west it frequents the coasts of Ecuador, Peru and Chile, including oceanic islands such as the Galapagos. The Chilean race is considered by some to be a separate species as it is a much larger bird than its northern relatives, being up to 6 feet in length, some 2 feet longer than those in the north.

Depending on the area, nests may be found either in trees — mangrove swamps are a favorite spot — or on the ground. If it is in a tree, then a rough platform of large twigs is constructed, while a scrape with some feathers as lining suffices on the ground. Nests are often packed densely together, with only enough room between each to ensure that physical contact

Chilean Pelican (top) and
Brown Pelican (bottom)

Brown
Chilean

Distribution of Chilean and Brown Pelicans

between the incubating birds is avoided.

The courtship activities of the Brown Pelican have been described as a very somber affair. The male circles the squatting female, lifting his wings and stretching his neck, all in silence. Finally the female flies out to sea, followed by the male, and mating takes place on the water.

The nesting season is somewhat irregular, varying from site to site and even at the same site from year to year. Three eggs are generally laid, and both parents take part in the incubation, which takes some 28 days. As with other species, the chicks are naked and helpless at first, but with the rich fish food they grow rapidly. Their food call is a piercing scream. Chicks on the ground roam about a good deal after several weeks in the nest, while those in trees are much more restricted. They are able to climb down when they are seven weeks old, though before then many will have fallen to their death; mortality among tree-nesters is high.

The Chilean subspecies is one of the guano birds (others are mentioned on pages 28 to 29, 72 to 73 and 92 to 93). It is not nearly so numerous as the other species, among which it nests. By virtue of its large size, however, it finds no difficulty in acquiring a nest site among the teeming multitudes.

Jaegers

The jaegers, or skuas, as they are known elsewhere, are a small family—the Stercorariidae—closely allied to the gulls. Four species are found in the Northern Hemisphere, one of which, the Great Skua *(Catharacta skua)*, is seen only rarely along the northern coasts of North America. It is widely distributed

Great Skua chasing a Kittiwake

in the Southern Hemisphere, with a number of subspecies from Chile eastward along the edge of the Antarctic continent and its islands to New Zealand.

The Great Skua, a heavily built bird about 23 inches in length, may easily be distinguished from brown immature gulls by its build and the prominent white wing patches which are visible during flight. It is more of a scavenger than the other species, frequently following ships and fishing fleets. It will also kill both chicks and adult birds of smaller species, besides being a great egg stealer. In the south, nests are often situated close to penguin colonies, which afford an easy food supply.

In Great Britain there has been a marked increase in this species during the last 50 years or so. For a time in the last century it was restricted to the Shetland Islands. However, since about 1920 it has increased in numbers and has spread south, now nesting in the Orkney Islands, Caithness, Sutherland and the Outer Hebrides, including St. Kilda. It has been suggested that during this expansion the Iceland population has decreased, so that there has been a shift in the breeding range toward the south rather than an overall increase in numbers.

Of the other species the Pomarine Jaeger (*Stercorarius pomarinus*) is the largest, being some 21 inches in length, and may be distinguished by its size, larger bill and curiously twisted central tail feathers. It nests on the tundras of northern Siberia, various Arctic islands, Greenland, northern Canada and Alaska.

The smallest species, the Long-tailed Jaeger (*S. longicaudus*), has central tail feathers extending some 8 inches beyond its body, making a total length of 20 inches. Its breeding range is circumpolar, extending farther north than any other jaeger, though also reaching far south in some regions. It is a thinly scattered species throughout its range and for successful breeding seems dependent on lemmings, its chief source of food.

The Parasitic Jaeger (*S. parasiticus*) is perhaps the most common jaeger species. It breeds along the coasts and islands of the polar basin, extending southward through the Aleutian Islands and, in Europe, to southern Scotland.

101

During the winter months, part of the Parasitic Jaeger population moves as far south as California along the Pacific coast, and from New England to Brazil along the Atlantic. European birds are sometimes seen as far south as the Cape of Good Hope and Australia.

As its name suggests, this species is dependent to a considerable extent on others for food. This it obtains by harrying, though rarely coming into actual physical contact with, species like terns and gulls. After sometimes only the briefest of chases, the victim will drop or disgorge its food and continue unmolested while the jaeger swoops down to feed.

In each of the three species of jaeger—the Pomarine, the Long-tailed and the Parasitic—light and dark, or color, phases occur, ranging from light through intermediate to dark-colored birds. The term polymorphism is used to denote this

Parasitic Jaeger in light phase (left), dark (center) and intermediate color phase (right)

phenomenon. Polymorphic traits are those which often show clinical variation (see page 16). For example, British ornithologists working in the Shetland Islands recently estimated that no more than between 25 and 30 percent of the Parasitic Jaeger population on the islands was pale phase. However, the percentage of pale-phase birds increases as one moves north through the birds' range.

In the Parasitic Jaeger, both dark and light forms occur, together with intermediates; these have received particular attention because of the counting of the phases throughout the birds' range. Although the phases readily interbreed, there is a tendency for birds to mate with those of the same color. For instance, Richard Perry, making observations on Noss, Shetland, noted that 21 matings were between dark pairs, 7 between light pairs and 9 were mixed matings. Similar observations have since been made at other colonies.

Long-tailed Jaeger

Jaegers breed either in loose colonies or individually, usually on bleak moorland and tundra. Some colonies may be very large; that of the Great Skua on Foula contains about 900 pairs. The nest is a depression in the ground or is made of vegetation, lined with dry grass and an occasional feather.

The two or three eggs take about 23 days to hatch in the case of the Long-tailed Jaeger and 28 days for the Great Skua. Both parents take a share in the incubation, the off-duty bird often standing guard close by. Any intruder in the nesting area, including man himself, is mobbed and chased vigorously.

The chicks, which are covered at first with brown down, are quite active and within several days leave the nest to hide nearby. During the breeding season, Parasitic Jaegers will often try to lure a chick away from the nest area by means of a distraction display, flapping about on the ground nearby as

Breeding range and winter distribution of Long-tailed Jaeger

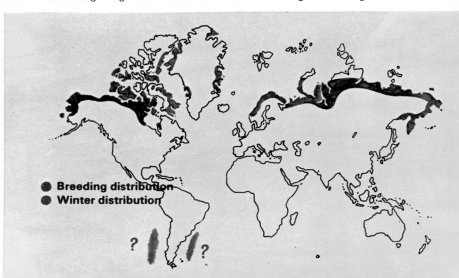

● **Breeding distribution**
● **Winter distribution**

if injured. The chicks are able to fly by the time they are about seven weeks old, but for two weeks more they may choose to remain dependent on their parents for support.

Jaegers are great wanderers during the off-season. The southern race of the Great Skua comes north into tropical waters, some crossing the Equator to appear off Japan and British Columbia, while one banded in Scotland was recovered in the French West Indies. The northern race frequents the North Atlantic; it was thought not to go beyond the Tropic of Capricorn, though the recent recovery of a Foula-banded bird from Guyana alters this idea.

Parasitic Jaegers have a transequatorial migration, with recoveries of banded birds being reported from both shores of the South Atlantic. Long-tailed Jaegers also move south to that area and are reported from South American waters in particular.

Pomarine Jaeger

Breeding range and winter distribution of Pomarine Jaeger

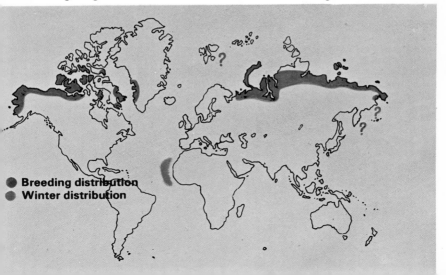

● **Breeding distribution**
● **Winter distribution**

Ring-billed Gull
in flight

Gulls

Gulls must be about the most familiar of all sea birds, though many species spend much of their life inland. Some may breed inland and winter on the coast. Saunders' Gull *(Larus saundersi)*, for example, nests on lakes in Mongolia but winters on the coast of Korea and China. Others such as the Black-legged Kittiwake *(Rissa tridactyla)* are much more oceanic.

The 44 species are distributed throughout the world, from the high Arctic to the snowy vastness of Antarctica.

Ring-billed Gull at rest

Some are widespread; the Mew Gull *(L. canus)*, for instance, nests in a range that extends across much of northern Europe, Asia and Canada. Others, such as Audouin's Gull of the Mediterranean (see pages 12 and 13) and the Swallow-tailed Gull *(Creagrus furcatus)* of the Galapagos, are very restricted in their range.

Gulls are generally noisy species, especially at nesting colonies, where the slightest disturbance will unleash a sound which is almost deafening. In size, the species range from the Greater Black-backed Gull *(L. marinus)*, a majestic bird some 30 inches in length, to the Little Gull *(L. minutus)*, a bare 10 inches. All species are stoutly built with long wings and short tails. They are excellent flyers and take every advantage of updrafts and eddies in order to effect flight with a minimum of effort. They will glide almost motionless in the slip stream of a ship or circle high in a thermal while flying home to roost.

Gulls may be divided into three distinct groups: the large white-headed gulls, a typical representative being the Ring-billed Gull *(L. delawarensis)*, which breeds on lakes in Canada and the northwestern United States; the hooded gulls, which include all those species with a dark head and of which the Sabine's Gull *(Xema sabini)* is a northern example; and the all-white gulls, of which the Ivory Gull is the solitary representative. It breeds on islands close to the Arctic pack ice, and is only a rare straggler farther south; even in the Polar winter it does not stray far beyond the ice limit.

Ivory Gull

Gulls are chiefly colonial nesters. Some colonies are very large, like that on Walney Island, England, which in 1969 contained some 17,500 pairs of Lesser Black-backed Gulls *(L. fuscus)* and 17,000 pairs of Herring Gulls. Other species may also nest in colonies, though at times they are more scattered. Nest sites vary a good deal with the habitat. Most are on the ground, but Bonaparte's Gull *(L. philadelphia)* may use a tree site. Nests may be placed in tussocks of grass or among floating vegetation; other sites may be on cliff ledges or in sand dunes, or occasionally in buildings.

Nests are composed of dry vegetation, feathers, small bones and other debris found close at hand. Quite a bulky structure may result, and in some cases the same site may be used, with additions, for several seasons. Two or three eggs are laid that are normally brown or green in color, blotched and

Young Great Black-backed Gull in second winter plumage (top) and juvenile (bottom)

Adult Great Black-backed Gull and chick

speckled with darker markings. Both sexes take part in the incubation which, depending on the species, takes up to four weeks. Should the clutch be lost during the early stages the bird will lay again after an interval, sometimes using the same nest or perhaps moving to a completely new one. If an egg is removed during the actual laying period, it will be replaced several times, even, it is said, up to 15 times.

The newly hatched chicks are covered with speckled brown down and leave the nest within a day or so. They are particularly difficult to find, as their 'camouflage' makes them almost invisible. They lose the down within several weeks, and in their juvenile plumage look bedraggled and ugly. The precise fledging time is often difficult to assess because the young hide or, if disturbed, move well away from the nest site. However, from a number of species that have been studied, it seems to be about seven weeks. Young gulls do not mature for several years; in the case of the Greater Black-backed Gull, four years elapse before full adult plumage is attained.

The Black-legged Kittiwake *(Rissa tridactyla)* and Red-legged Kittiwake *(R. brevirostris)* are among the most maritime gulls. The former nests on sea cliffs along many coasts in North America, northern Europe and Asia, while the latter is restricted to islands in the Bering Sea.

Both species are oceanic in their habits, coming ashore only to nest and spending the off-season roaming the northern oceans. The Black-legged Kittiwake, as indicated by many recoveries of birds banded in Great Britain, habitually crosses the North Atlantic and is found off eastern Canada and along the west coast of Greenland.

Kittiwakes normally nest on steep cliffs, where their relatively large nests adhere to the smallest ledges and rock niches. Occasionally there are records of birds nesting in areas of sand dunes or even on top of a discarded oil drum, but the most significant change seems to have taken place within recent years in Great Britain. There the number of birds has increased remarkably, with many new colonies being established. Lower, more accessible cliffs are now being used, along with such artificial sites as harbor walls, a seaside pier and a warehouse. The warehouse is in Dunbar, Scotland, where the colony nesting on the window ledges must be about the easiest of all sea bird colonies to count!

Besides this move to more manmade sites, birds have moved inland for several miles to nest on riverside buildings on the Tyne, a heavily polluted and industrialized river. Birds in the same area have been observed feeding on bread and scraps being thrown to other species. These developments would seem to indicate that a marked change is possible in the habits of the Black-legged Kittiwake, though whether this will occur is certainly an open question.

Nesting in confined situations, the Black-legged Kittiwake does show several adaptations to its environment. The normal clutch size has declined to two, as a larger number of chicks would not be possible in the confined space. The chicks remain almost stationary on the nest; and if the nest is on level ground they do not leave to take shelter, as do the chicks of other gull species, when danger threatens.

Kittiwake and chicks (nest on warehouse window-ledge)

their territories. As these are only used for nesting and not as feeding areas, the pieces of ground occupied may be quite small. The females are gradually attracted in; as the same pieces of ground may be occupied for a period of years, it often happens that the same pairs are formed. This probably also happens in many other sea bird species. Experiments have shown that Herring Gulls are able to recognize their mates at 30 yards but are unable to recognize their eggs. In fact, they will sit on anything that is even only an approximation of the size and shape of an egg!

The territory is guarded from all intruders by the holder's use of various displays and threat postures. Although the colony may be divided up quite haphazardly into territories, by the time the eggs are laid each bird knows its neighbors and the limits of its own area, and intruders are rapidly driven off. Chicks which remain in their territory are relatively safe, but those that stray are generally killed by neighboring adults.

Much interesting work using model bills has been done with chicks. It has been shown conclusively that the red spot near the tip of an adult's yellow bill acts as a stimulus to the chicks to beg for food. Little reaction is evoked by a bill where this spot has been erased. The fact that the chicks beg for food on catching sight of the red bill also promotes the reaction in the adults of feeding them.

Chick pecking at artificial beak

Black-headed Gull and chicks

The Black-headed Gull *(L. ridibundus)*, another wide-spread species, has also received a good deal of attention from ornithologists interested in bird behavior. In 1937 Kirkman's *Bird Behaviour* was published in England; it was based mainly on work upon this species of gull.

In more recent years experiments and observations of this species have been made by the famous animal behaviorist, Niko Tinbergen and students at the Ravenglass Nature Reserve, Cumberland, England. Some 10,000 pairs nested there in 1969.

One aspect studied was the method of eggshell removal from the nest. It has been shown that an empty eggshell placed

Selecting discarded eggshells from unhatched and hatching eggs

close to an egg on the open beach means that the egg will be more vulnerable to predation by other gulls and the Carrion Crow. It would seem, therefore, that the removal of eggshells from the vicinity of the nest is of particular importance in curtailing the amount of predation on unhatched eggs or small chicks.

It has been observed that a gull will roll an egg back into the nest but will quickly remove a shell. What are the characteristics which enable shells to be distinguished from the unhatched egg? Six were listed, of which five were distinguishable by sight; the sixth was weight and could only be distinguished by actually moving the egg or shell.

Various experiments were carried out in order to see how recognition is achieved, using a number of model eggs and shells. It was found that the factors which lead to shell removal are that a broken shell has a thin, serrated edge and shows white inside, whereas a whole egg has no edge, a smooth outline and shows no white, being brown with black markings. In addition, the gull tests an eggshell for weight; should it be significantly above that of an empty shell, the impulse to remove it will be checked. This act prevents chicks which have hatched but have not yet completely left the shell from being carried away in error.

In many parts of the world the numbers of gulls have increased dramatically, often to the detriment of other species. Much of this increase seems attributable to the amount of waste material available, not only in garbage dumps and in river systems but also discarded by fishing fleets at sea. A few years ago, for example, a landfill project was undertaken in Juneau, Alaska, using the city's refuse. Plans called for covering the garbage with soil as soon as it was dumped. This was not done, however, and the gull population soared.

Whether the gull population would decrease if such alternative sources of food were removed is a debatable point. From the evidence so far available, it seems that these highly adaptable birds would find other means of supply, and they are, of course, also capable of fishing for themselves.

One of the difficulties of containing gull populations, once they have gotten out of hand, is the fact that gull species are exceptionally long lived and do not need a high percentage of reproductive success to maintain their numbers. In addition, these birds are protected in the United States by federal laws.

Similar problems are being encountered in Britain, since gulls are extending both their winter and breeding ranges southward along both sides of the Atlantic. In Britain, the increase in gulls seems to have begun long ago, during the latter half of the 19th century, when the first bird protection acts began to have an effect. At the same time the human population of some remote islands was declining, and in certain cases even being evacuated completely; there was also less of a need to live far from the land. Thus predation by man on sea bird colonies decreased.

Gulls are a particular menace to other sea birds, especially to Manx Shearwaters and puffins. At one Welsh colony, the shearwater comprised some 45 percent of the gulls' food during the breeding season, a state of affairs that had to be checked, to some extent at least, by control measures. In this case a trapping campaign was started.

Young Manx Shearwaters comprise the largest percentage of the Great Black-backed Gull's diet.

Food of Great Black-backed Gull

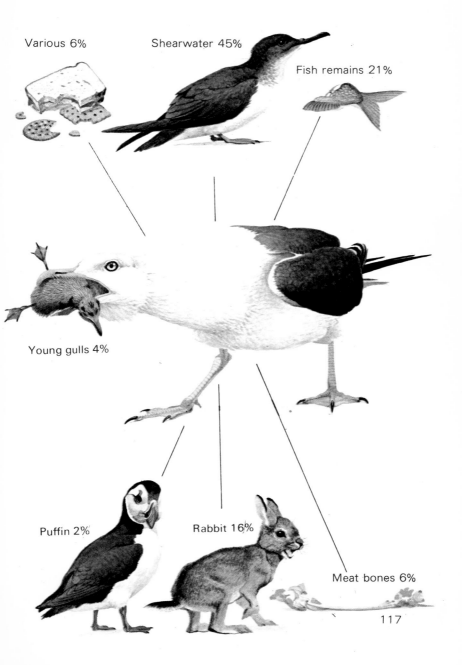

Various 6%

Shearwater 45%

Fish remains 21%

Young gulls 4%

Puffin 2%

Rabbit 16%

Meat bones 6%

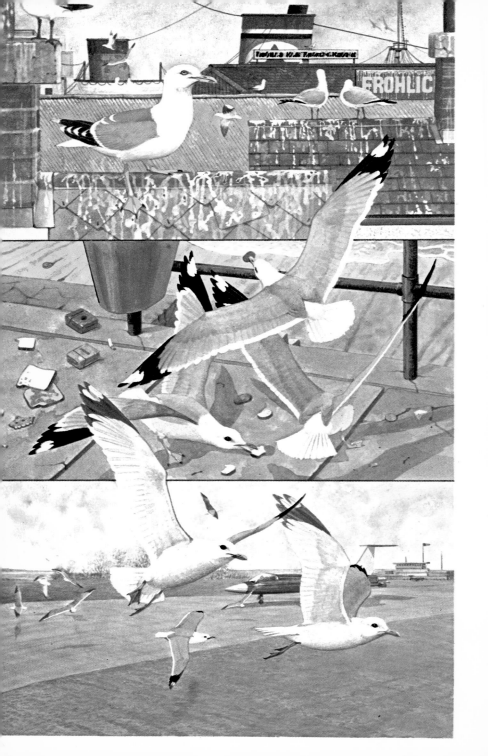

The increase of gulls has brought about a number of problems, one of which, as we have just mentioned, is predation on smaller sea birds. The arrival of some species may literally wipe out others. This is of particular importance in the case of tern colonies, which have suffered in some areas through the sudden expansion in gull numbers.

An Avocet colony in Great Britain, a reserve of the Royal Society for the Protection of Birds, was threatened by Black-headed Gulls which were taking virtually all the season's production of chicks. The gulls were eventually driven off after their nests had been continually raked out; predation has now been greatly minimized. In the Camargue, narcotic baits have been used with effect against predatory Herring Gulls, and in Holland a campaign using strychnine against the same species has had a limited effect in containing the population. Other methods have been tried, including sterilization of both adults and eggs. Gulls, being very long-lived species, need to produce very few chicks during their lifetime in order to keep a stable population. Any control, therefore, must of necessity be wide-ranging and efficient in order to have the desired effect.

Gulls are a particular nuisance at airfields, where they often congregate to feed or rest. This creates quite a problem, as aircraft collisions with birds are very dangerous during take-offs and landings. It is difficult to estimate the cost of the damage done to aircraft by gulls; however, it is no mere coincidence that reports of 'strikes', as they are called by aviators, are frequent at all coastal airports. At one time, serious gull problems were experienced at Logan International Airport near Boston, Massachusetts. In Britain, the Royal Air Force estimates that damage done to its planes by gulls amounts to nearly 250 million dollars each year.

Gulls habitually using reservoirs may pollute them with *Salmonella* picked up through feeding in garbage dumps and around sewage-pipe outlets. They may possibly transmit avian tuberculosis to cattle, and have also been associated with the spread of bovine cysticercosis.

A new and growing habit is that of nesting on buildings,

Herring Gulls (top and center) and Mew Gulls (bottom)

particularly in coastal towns. They foul buildings and pavements, and the noise they create is a considerable nuisance early in the morning. This new menace could create more serious problems than city pigeons or starlings.

Two species of gulls inhabit the high Arctic regions in addition to the Ivory Gull (see pages 106 to 107). These are Sabine's Gull *(Xema sabini)* and Ross's Gull *(Rhodosethia rosea),* both of which are interesting though little-known birds.

Sabine's Gull was first discovered by a member of John Ross's first Arctic expedition in 1818 on islands in Melville Bay, northwestern Greenland. The discoverer, E. Sabine, also gave his name to the islands.

The Sabine's Gull is probably the most ternlike of all gulls, with a light, buoyant flight and a grating, ternlike cry. It breeds in marshy areas, often close to Arctic Tern colonies, in Alaska, Arctic Canada, Greenland and Arctic Siberia. The nest is a mere hollow lined with grass, and two or three eggs are laid. The winter range is not fully known. There is a small autumn passage southward off western European coasts,

Sabine's Gull

but records of its spring range are few.

Ross's Gull is a much rarer visitor to northern Alaska and northern Canada. Although first discovered by James Clark Ross, at the time a member of Parry's second expedition in search of the Northwest Passage in 1823, the next 50 or so years produced very few additional records and no sign of a nesting site.

Explorers on board the ill-fated 'Jeanette', trapped in pack ice north of Siberia, saw numbers of these birds and more skins were procured. Three were brought out by one of the survivors, who carried them beneath his shirt across the pack ice after the ship was crushed in the floe. Other explorers amid the polar ice, including Nansen, encountered more birds. It was not until 1905, however, that a nest was found — by S. A. Buterlin in the delta of the Kolyma River in eastern Siberia. Although these birds are seen in Alaska and northern Canada, it seems as though the only nesting area is among the clumps of rough grass on boggy marshes in the river valleys close to the tree line of northern Siberia.

Terns

Like their close relatives the gulls, the terns, or Sternidae, are a large group of almost worldwide distribution, their main stronghold being the Pacific Basin. There are some 39 species and many subspecies, one of the largest being the Crested Tern *(Sterna bernsteini)*, some 21 inches in length, which is common in the Indian Ocean and western Pacific. There are a number of very small species little more than 8 or 9 inches in length, including the Damara Tern *(S. balaenarum)* of South African waters and the Amazon Tern *(S. superci-*

Roseate Tern in flight

liaris) of South American river systems.

Terns are slender birds with long wings and forked tails, giving rise to the common name 'sea-swallows'. The bill is generally long and slender though in some species, notably the Gull-billed Tern *(Gelochelidon nilotica)*, it is much more ponderous. Both the bill and legs may be brightly colored, usually red, yellow or black, or a combination of these.

Fish and small invertebrates are the main food; they

Roseate Tern on its nest

are caught by the birds swooping down, often plunging partly beneath the surface in order to effect a capture. While fishing, they hold their heads down and hover in flight in a characteristic manner. Although they have webbed feet, terns only rarely swim or rest on the water, preferring to stand on a beach or a convenient floating object.

They may be divided broadly into three main groups. The black-capped terns, containing over 30 species, including the Roseate Tern. *(Sterna dougallii)*, are found in all oceans and on many inland river and lake systems. The noddy terns comprise a group of five species found only in tropical regions: two are dark in color, two intermediate and one mainly white. There is only a solitary representative in the last group, the Inca Tern *(Larosterna inca)*, which is found on islands off the coasts of southern Peru and Chile.

When nesting, terns are very gregarious and some colonies are of tremendous size. A colony of the Sooty Tern *(S. fuscata)* in the Seychelles was believed to contain 5 million pairs some 30 years ago. A more recent survey on the same island gave the population as 1.2 million pairs, which worked out at an average density of two and a half pairs per square yard, with over three pairs per square yard in suitable places.

Fairy Tern and egg

Sooty Tern and chick (bottom left) and Inca Tern at nest (bottom right)

Just as the species are varied in their breeding habits, so are the nesting sites which they use. Birds nesting on open shingle beaches or on sand dunes make do with the barest of scrapes. Some of the marsh terns construct nests of floating vegetation which may either float themselves or be placed on mounds of floating debris. The Common Noddy *(Anous stolidus)* builds untidy nests of seaweed in low bushes and shrubs. The Fairy Tern, or White Noddy *(A. alba),* lays a single egg balanced on the branch of a tree or on a rock ledge. The chick is adapted for such a precarious existence in that it can hang upside down if necessary, holding on by its claws.

The Sooty Tern breeds mainly on islands in the Caribbean, Atlantic, Indian and Pacific Oceans. It has received particular attention in the colony known as 'Wideawake Fair' on Ascension Island. The bird has been called the 'Wideawake Tern' because of its perpetual screaming 'ker-wacky-wack', which may be heard at any time of the day or night. The Sooty Tern on Ascension has a breeding cycle of nine and a half months, but elsewhere the cycle is the normal 12 months. On Ascension the birds spend six or seven months at the colony, then disappear to sea for three months. The incubation period is about 30 days and fledging is at about five weeks, but the chicks remain in the area for eight weeks more.

Common Noddy at nest

Three species of terns are usually referred to as 'marsh terns'. The Black Tern *(Chlidonias niger)* breeds in Europe south of the Baltic and eastward across central Asia, and also occurs in the central United States and southern Canada. The White-winged Black Tern *(C. leucopterus)* nests eastward from Hungary to the shores of the China Sea, though in central Asia its range is discontinuous. There have been many sporadic cases of nesting just beyond the edge of its range and many suspected attempts, particularly in the Mediterranean region and in Africa, where there is a distinct possibility that breeding colonies await discovery. The Whiskered Tern *(C. hybrida)* breeds in a number of areas from southern Spain eastward to India, Australia and New Zealand, and also in southern Africa.

The breeding habits of the White-winged Black Tern are still far from clear. It arrives late in the season, up to three weeks after the Black Tern in the same area. Although it sometimes nests with other marsh species, it tends to keep apart and form subcolonies. The nest is a platform of reeds plucked by the birds and built up above the water level. Black Terns' nests are much smaller affairs, usually made of decaying vegetation; they may even be constructed of floating debris. Whiskered Terns' nests are loosely made heaps of reed stems, and may be either afloat or placed in clumps of vegetation. Very little care is taken in nest-building and the structures fall apart quite easily. Though attempts are made to pluck growing reeds these meet with little success, and the birds make use of pieces broken off during the passage of larger animals.

Besides the marsh terns several other species spend most of their time on inland lakes and rivers, rarely going to the sea. Forster's Tern *(S. forsteri)* breeds mainly on inland lakes in western Canada and the United States and moves south to Central America during the winter. It returns to its northern breeding grounds during the early spring to feed on dead fish and invertebrates released by the melting ice. The Indian River Tern *(S. aurantia)* is found on many lakes from Iran and Iraq eastward to Burma and the Malay Peninsula. Found in virtually the same area as the Indian River Tern, and often seen with it, is the Black-bellied Tern *(S. melanogastes)*.

(Top to bottom) Black Tern, Indian River Tern and Whiskered Tern

One of the greatest bird wanderers is the Arctic Tern (*S. paradisaea*), which nests in a great circumpolar arc in the Arctic regions. It ranges to within eight degrees of the North Pole, though at the same time it extends its breeding range southward to Massachusetts on the western Atlantic and to Great Britain and northern France in the eastern side. Although a coastal bird, it is also found far inland on moors and tundra and the gravel beaches of lakes and rivers.

The terns return to their nesting grounds during April and May. If the Arctic Tern is in a mixed ternery—as the colony is called when several species breed together—it will choose the barest ground, though in the absence of competition for nest sites it will use any suitable spot. The size of a colony may vary from one or two pairs nesting on a small rock to many hundreds scattered over a larger island or tract of marsh land.

British studies on the Farne Islands reveal that no Arctic Terns under three years of age nest, while those doing so for the first time are generally unsuccessful. Those achieving the greatest breeding success are between five or ten years old, though some birds live for as long as 20 years. The incuba-

Breeding range, banded recoveries and sight records of Arctic Tern

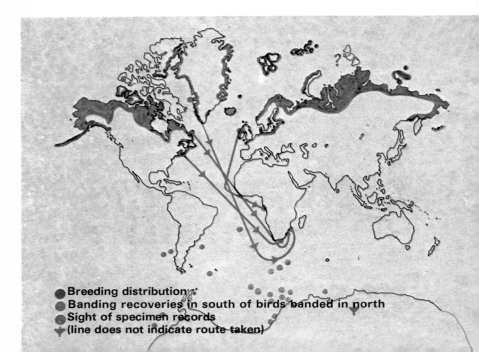

Breeding distribution
Banding recoveries in south of birds banded in north
Sight of specimen records
(line does not indicate route taken)

Arctic Tern and chicks

tion period is about three weeks and fledging about four weeks. Where colonies are sited on the coast, the birds feed on small fish and crustaceans, but if they are inland a wide variety of insect life is also taken.

During the autumn the birds begin their transequatorial migration which takes them to Antarctic regions. It has been said that some Arctic Terns enjoy more hours of daylight than any other animal, for they live during the summer in the land of the midnight sun and many spend the rest of the year in the unending daylight of an Antarctic summer. The journeys undertaken twice yearly by the Arctic Tern will often be 8,000 miles and may reach 11,000 in some cases, a unique undertaking for such a small bird or, indeed, for any bird.

The Sandwich Tern *(Thalasseus sandvicencis)* is only found along the coasts of the United States and Mexico from North Carolina southward, on European coasts from southern Sweden southward and in the Black and Caspian Seas. Its major European stronghold in the past was Holland, where it is estimated that in the years prior to 1955 between 30,000 and 40,000 pairs nested. This was believed to represent half the European population of the species. Since that date the Dutch population has slumped dramatically to about 500 pairs. It is thought that pesticide residues, found in eggs and dead birds, have been an important contributory factor in this decline.

In North America, Sandwich Terns breed in colonies on sandy beaches from the Carolinas south to Florida and around the Gulf of Mexico as far west as Texas. They lay two or three eggs which are highly variable in color. Unlike other tern species, both parents constantly alternate sitting on the nest

Protective measure used in Least Tern nesting colony, at Gibraltar Point, Lincs, England

Sandwich Tern

during the incubation period.

The Least Tern (S. *albifrons*) is widespread throughout the world, living in all continents except South America, and is as much at home on lakes and rivers hundreds of miles inland as it is on the coast.

In 1903, when wardens from the National Audubon Society first patrolled the North Carolina coast, there were only 16 eggs reported from the several Least Tern colonies visited. Under protection from feather-hunters since that time, this diminutive sea bird has increased its numbers in the United States.

A British survey made in 1967 showed a total British population of only 1,600 pairs. Protection of the bird has now been established in parts of that country.

Skimmers

Allied to the terns and gulls is an interesting small group of three species, the skimmers, or scissor bills. The Black Skimmer *(Rynchops nigra)*, the largest, is some 20 inches in length. It is found nesting along the coasts of the United States from New Jersey to Texas and on many coasts in South America southward to Argentina. The African Skimmer *(R. flavirostris)*, about 17 inches in length, is found both on the coasts and inland water systems of Africa, from the Red Sea south to the Orange River. It is no longer found in the Nile Valley. The Indian Skimmer *(R. albicollis)*, of similar size to the last species, inhabits on the rivers and large lakes of Burma and India.

The eye of the skimmer is unique among birds, its pupil being a vertical slit like that of a cat, but the most remarkable feature of these species is its large bill. When the chick hatches, both mandibles are the same length and can be used to pick up food in the normal manner. However, as the young begin to approach the flying stage the typical adult bill develops. In this, the upper mandible is distinctly shorter than the lower, which is very flexible.

The birds rarely alight on the surface of the water but catch their prey, small fish and surface-dwelling aquatic inverte-

Detail of skimmer's bill (left) and in flight 'skimming' (right)

brates, as they fly along very low with the bill open and the lower mandible scooping through the water for several yards. Feeding is normally undertaken at dawn or dusk and during the night when the moon is full. For efficient feeding calm water is essential, and birds may completely desert a river during times of flooding.

Skimmers form colonies, though most of them are small. A typical site is a sand bank where a slight hollow is scooped out for use as a nest. Up to four eggs may be laid; both parents take part in the incubation. The chicks, which can swim well, leave the nest after hatching.

(Top to bottom) Black Skimmer, African Skimmer and Indian Skimmer

Auks in the North Atlantic and North Pacific

Razorbill

Common Guillemot

Brünnich's Guillemot

Little Auk or Dovekie

Black Guillemot

Spectacled Guillemot

Pigeon Guillemot

Marbled Murrelet

Kittlitz's Murrelet

Cassin's Auklet

Parakeet Auklet

Crested Auklet

Least Auklet

Whiskered Auklet

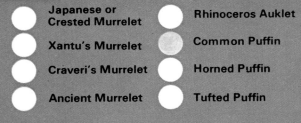

Japanese or Crested Murrelet

Xantu's Murrelet

Craveri's Murrelet

Ancient Murrelet

Rhinoceros Auklet

Common Puffin

Horned Puffin

Tufted Puffin

Auks

The family of auks, or Alcidae, are restricted to the colder regions of the Northern Hemisphere, with no representatives in the Southern. Here their place is taken by the penguins (see pages 18 to 29) and diving petrels (see pages 60 to 63). The majority of species live in the North Pacific and Bering Sea and 16 are restricted entirely to these areas. Only six species are found in the North Atlantic, of which three are endemic.

The auks may be divided into seven groups or tribes. The tribe Alcini contains the Razorbill, or Razor-billed Auk *(Alca torda)*, and the two murres, or guillemots, the Common Guillemot *(Uria aalge)* and Brünnich's Guillemot *(U. lomvia)*. The latter species are found in both oceans; the Razorbill, only in the North Atlantic.

A single species, the Little Auk, or Dovekie *(Plautus alle)*, belongs to the tribe Plautini. This bird is about 8 inches in length and breeds in Arctic Canada, Greenland, Iceland, Novaya Zemblya, Spitzbergen and Franz Josef Land. Some colonies of this bird, perhaps the most numerous bird in the North Atlantic, are small, but others are immense. The colony near Thule, Greenland, contains well over a million pairs. With myriads of birds flying and gliding past a cliff, it is very difficult to obtain good estimates of the number present.

The Black Guillemot *(Cepphus grylle)*, Pigeon Guillemot *(C. columba)* — sometimes considered only as a race of the former species — and the Spectacled Guillemot *(C. carbo)* are members of the tribe Cepphini.

The three species of puffins, two living in the North Pacific and the third in the North Atlantic, belong to the tribe Fraterculini. Closely related to them are the auklets of the North Pacific, the five species of the tribe Aethini.

The last two tribes are both comprised of murrelets, species which are also found only in the North Pacific and Bering Sea area. The tribe Brachyramphini has two species, the Marbled Murrelet *(Brachyramphus marmoratus)* and Kittliz's Murrelet *(B. brevirostre)*. The tribe Synthliboramphini contains the remaining four species.

Distribution of the auk family

The Great Auk *(Pinguinis impennis)*, or the Garefowl, as it is sometimes known, is, or rather was, the largest of its family — unfortunately it has been extinct for over a century. Standing some 30 inches high, the Great Auk resembled a giant Razorbill except that it was flightless, a fact which helped to spell its doom. It was the original 'penguin', a name which was handed on later to that well-known group of birds from the Southern Hemisphere.

From the remains of the Great Auk found in numerous cave deposits and kitchen middens throughout northwestern Europe and the Mediterranean region, it is evident that this bird was formerly a source of food.

Only eight breeding places of the Great Auk have been discovered while about a dozen further sites are suspected. Undoubtedly the birds also nested elsewhere. The main population center may once have been in the Newfoundland area, judging by the reports of explorers like Jacques Cartier, who arrived in the region in 1534. Later accounts tell of birds being taken by the boatload for food by ships' crews, the hapless auks being driven up planks or across sails straight on board the vessels. The slaughter was so immense that by about 1800 the Great Auk was extinct as a breeding bird in Newfoundland.

In Europe the Great Auk nested on St. Kilda until the latter half of the 17th century; a tutor to the lord of the island has left a description of the bird and its habits. It was on one of the great sea stacks of St. Kilda, Stac an Armin, that in 1840 the last Great Auk to be seen alive in British waters was clubbed to death by two islanders who thought they had en-

Breeding areas of the Great Auk

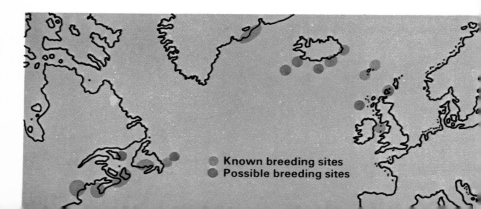

Known breeding sites
Possible breeding sites

countered a witch. It would seem, therefore, that well before that date the unfortunate bird was already a most unusual occurrence in those waters.

The doom of the Great Auk was finally sealed on June 4th, 1844, on the island of Eldey, Iceland, when two Great Auks were killed and the single egg smashed. Since that day none has been seen alive, though many people searched for them during the mid-19th century, but without success. Man's ignorance and greed were responsible for the extermination of a remarkable species of sea bird.

Great Auk

Razorbill with chick

Most members of the family Alcidae are colonial species, and some congregate in immense colonies. A colony of Brünnich's Guillemot at Cape Shackleton, West Greenland, probably contains a million pairs, half the Greenland population of this bird. The Black Guillemot on the other hand, though it is found in small colonies, may often nest in solitary pairs with a considerable distance between each pair.

Nest sites vary; the Common and Brünnich's Guillemots use ledges, which are often exceedingly narrow, while the Razorbill prefers crevices and hollows beneath boulders. Others, notably the puffins, are burrow-nesters. One or two eggs are laid, depending on the species, and both parents take part in the incubation. Chicks are covered in down on hatching.

Xantu's Murrelet and chick (left) and Common Puffin with young (right)

Those of one of the murrelet tribes are truly remarkable in that they leave the nest when only a few days old to go to sea. Even at that early stage, they have enormous feet almost the size of their parents.

The chicks of other species, such as the Razorbill, stay on the nest ledge or crevice until they are between two and three weeks old and a third of the size of their parents. They usually leave it at dusk, urged down to the sea, perhaps hundreds of feet below, by the agitated cries of their parents swimming about on the water.

The chicks of the puffins, safe below ground in a burrow, take things much more leisurely and do not leave its safety until they are fully grown and feathered.

Horned Puffin (left)
and Tufted Puffin (right)

The Common, or Atlantic, Puffin *(Fratercula arctica)* lives in the North Atlantic, while the remaining two species, the Tufted Puffin *(Lunda cirrhata)* and the Horned Puffin *(F. corniculata)*, are found in the North Pacific.

Puffins are comical birds, always curious about what their neighbors are doing. This often leads to duels when their huge beaks are used to grip on opponent's leg or wing. These encounters may be very prolonged; if they are near a cliff edge, both birds may fall over, only to break apart before reaching the rocks or sea below.

Not only does the Horned Puffin quarrel with others, it also seems to carry on a protracted argument with its mate. Such arguments are often carried on in the nest chamber from which angry growling and scolding noises may be heard.

Common Puffin
and map showing
breeding areas

The Common Guillemot, or Murre, is a species which, at least in the eastern Atlantic, seems to be decreasing at many colonies, particularly those in the southern section of its range. Changes in temperature, which in turn affect the food supply, and pollution of the sea are major contributory factors in this decline.

Although their breeding season is relatively short—approximately May to July—Guillemots visit the cliffs over a much wider period. Probably the only months when they do not land are August (except for delayed breeders), September and October. During the winter months, in suitably calm weather, large numbers of the birds will visit the colony in the hours soon after dawn, often for only a brief time. These irregular visits, which continue with increasing regularity until the onset of breeding, are still the subject of speculation among ornithologists.

The Common Guillemot occurs in two forms, the normal and the 'ringed', or 'bridled', form. The Bridled Guillemot was at one time erroneously believed to be a separate species. Since the 1930's several surveys into the range of the bridled form have been conducted by H. N. Southern. They have established that the bridled form is absent from the Pacific Ocean, being found only in Atlantic colonies. Here the enquiries revealed that the percentage of bridled birds is one percent or less in the south of England and on the coasts of France. As colonies to the north are examined, it soon becomes apparent that the percentage increases, so that in southwestern Ireland over 50 percent of the birds are bridled.

Brünnich's Guillemot *(Uria lomvia)* grows to a length of about 18 inches. It is thought by some authorities that this bird resembles the penguins more than any other North American species. Brünnich's Guillemots live primarily in Greenland and Hudson Bay, although they have nested as far south as the Gulf of St. Lawrence.

The three species which make up the tribe Cepphini differ in a number of respects from others in the auk family. On land they do not stand nearly so upright, and when at rest their posture is almost duck-like. They have only weak, though often high-pitched, calls. The Spectacled, Pigeon and Black

Common Guillemot (top), Brünnich's Guillemot (bottom left) and
Bridled Guillemot (bottom right)

Guillemots, therefore, should not be confused with the
murres—Brünnich's Guillemot and the Common Guillemot—discussed on the previous pages.

The nest sites of guillemots are usually in crevices or
among boulders on rocky islands and coastlines. These birds
do not attempt to construct a nest, but instead lay their

Spectacled Guillemot (left) and Pigeon Guillemot (right)

two or three eggs on the bare rock surface. The incubation period is between 27 and 30 days. The chicks remain at the nest site until they are about five weeks old and fully grown. Since guillemots do not nest in colonies, as do many other sea birds, not nearly so much is known about their numbers and distribution.

The Black Guillemot is a bird of Atlantic coastal waters. It breeds from southern Greenland south to Maine on the North Atlantic side and along the coast of Scotland, in the Shetlands and in the northern Irish Sea on the European side. By contrast, the Pigeon Guillemot inhabits northern Pacific

Little Auk (left) and Black Guillemot (right)

waters from the islands and coastlines of the Arctic Ocean, through the Bering Sea as far south as Catalina Island, California and northern Japan.

The Little Auk, in a tribe all on its own, nests in the Arctic regions in large colonies. These are usually found near the base of steep slopes, though the birds may go up beyond the snowline to a height of 1,500 feet. Other colonies may be on cliffs as much as 20 miles inland from the sea.

The birds move south during the winter, with huge numbers congregating on the Grand Banks, Newfoundland. Smaller numbers are found off western European coasts.

The murrelets, of which there are six species, belong to two tribes. All are small birds between 8 inches and 10 inches in length.

The Marbled Murrelet is still a bird of mystery, in that only a single egg has been found, and that was taken from the oviduct of a dead female. The nest sites have never been found, though the bird is numerous on the coasts of Alaska and British Columbia and in the islands eastward to Kamchatka. From the evidence, it seems that the birds fly inland, perhaps many miles, to nest in the high timberlands, but the virtual inaccessibility of the terrain makes the search for a colony tremendously difficult.

Kittlitz's Murrelet is another species that flies far inland to breed. It makes its nest on bare ground among rocks and snow in locations north of the timber line in Alaska and in the treeless islands across the North Pacific. A nest site of this species was not discovered until 1913.

The Japanese, or Crested, Murrelet *(Synthliboramphus wumizusume)* nests on the coasts of Japan. Xantu's Murrelet

Ancient Murrelet
(left) and
Marbled Murrelet
(right) in summer
plumage

(Endomychura hypoleuca) nests on islands off California. It lays one or two eggs in mid-March, using crevices among boulders or even the cover of dense bushes as nest sites. No material is used at the nest. Birds use suitable spots from just above the high-water mark to high up mountain sides. The young are led to sea by their parents within a few days of hatching, and even at this early stage can swim and dive with amazing skill.

Craveri's Murrelet *(E. craveri)* is considered by some authorities to be the southern race of the previous species. It nests on islands in the Gulf of California, where the breeding season begins in February, and, like Xantu's Murrelet, it is nocturnal at the breeding colonies.

The Ancient Murrelet *(S. antiquum)* resides much farther north in Alaska and across the Bering Sea. The nest is usually in a burrow, and two eggs are laid. Nocturnal at its breeding grounds, the Ancient Murrelet has a call similar to that of a Leach's Petrel, except that it is higher pitched.

Kittlitz's Murrelet in summer plumage

Cassin's Auklet (left), Rhinoceros Auklet (center) and Crested Auklet (right)

The six auklets are also small species. The Least Auklet *(Aethia pusilla)* is barely 7 inches in length, while the Rhinoceros Auklet *(Cerorhinca monocerata)* is the largest at 14 inches. This bird gets its name from the blunt horn at the base of the beak. During April, the birds return to their colonies along the western coasts of Canada and the United States as far south as the state of Washington and on islands as far west as Kamchatka. They are nocturnal birds when ashore and are noisy when they first arrive. Later, as the breeding season begins, the colonies are silent except for the whirring of the auklets' short wings. Their nests, lined with dead grass, are at the end of tunnels which may be up to 20 feet in length, though they are usually between 5 and 8 feet. A single egg is laid late in May.

The Crested Auklet *(A. cristatella)* breeds on the Pribilof, Aleutian and Shumagin Islands and in southwestern Alaska. Because of its flight, size and color it has received the local name 'sea-quail'. During May these auklets return to their breeding

Least Auklet (left), Parakeet
Auklet (center) and Whiskered
Auklet (right)

colonies, which are usually located on prominent headlands
having a conglomeration of boulders just above the high-
water mark. Both parents take turns in the incubation of the
single egg, the precise duration of which is not known. The
young remain hidden away until they can fly.

The Whiskered Auklet *(A. pygmaea)* is probably the rarest
and least known of the tribe. It nests in the Aleutian Islands
and is seldom seen any great distance from its colonies. The
Parakeet Auklet *(Cyclorrhynchus psittacula)* breeds from
northeastern Siberia through the Bering Sea islands to Alaska.
It is a very tame or, perhaps, fearless species which nests in
burrows among rocks.

Cassin's Auklet *(Ptychoramphus aleutica),* a nocturnal
species, has the widest breeding range of all, being found south
from the Aleutian Islands to central California. It is very
numerous on some islands, and nests not only in natural
crevices but under driftwood and even among sacks of coal.
It has a prolonged breeding season.

OTHER MARITIME SPECIES

In the preceding pages the groups of birds generally accepted as sea birds have been discussed. However, it is obvious that a number of species from different groups are far from oceanic in their habits. Some of the gulls and terns, in particular, are restricted to inland lakes and river systems.

There are, moreover, other birds which lay strong claim to be classified as sea birds, particularly the three species of phalarope. Wilson's Phalarope *(Steganopus tricolor)*, the largest at about 10 inches in length, is the least pelagic of the three. The other two species have different names on either side of the Atlantic, which can lead to confusion. The Red Phalarope *(Phalaropus fulicarius)*, named after its summer plumage, is called the Gray Phalarope in Europe, after its gray winter dress. The Northern Phalarope *(Lobipes lobatus)* of the United States becomes the Red-necked Phalarope in Europe. In this account the appropriate American names will be used.

Both species are circumpolar in their distribution, with some overlapping in range. However, the Northern extends farther south in summer than does the Red. All three species have an unusual spinning action when they are feeding. They turn around quickly on the water, picking up floating organisms and small invertebrates which are carried to the top by the turbulence the birds create.

Both the Northern and Red Phalaropes spend the winter at sea, moving southward in both the Pacific and Atlantic Oceans to areas having a rich plankton supply. The Northern is a more tropical species in winter, while the Red Phalarope continues south to temperate zones. Preferred winter areas for both species include an area off West Africa north of the Equator, off Angola and southwestern Africa, Peru, Arabian waters and the southwestern Pacific.

It is not surprising that such small birds, wandering the world's oceans, should occasionally suffer disasters when large numbers are carried on to coasts and inland by severe weather. In Newfoundland they are known by the local name 'gale-birds'.

Northern Phalarope

The duck family has among its many members several that are more or less maritime in their habits. In northern Europe one of the most frequent birds to be seen along rocky coasts is the Common Eider *(Somateria mollissima)*. It has a discontinuous circumpolar distribution going beyond 80 degrees north latitude in several places. In Europe there has been an expansion of range southward in recent years. The birds often congregate in large colonies; one colony in Greenland contains some 10,000 pairs. The down, which in Iceland is harvested from nests, is of the purest quality.

The three species of scoter are also largely marine, only coming ashore to nest. The Velvet Scoter *(Melanitta fusca)* has a circumpolar distribution though it rarely goes beyond the tree line. They breed on inland lakes, often in mountainous areas, but move to the sea during winter months. The Common Scoter *(Oidemia nigra)* is found throughout northern Europe and Asia and in Alaska. After the breeding season it spends all

its time at sea, normally in coastal areas where it feeds on bivalves taken from the floor of the ocean.

The four species of loon, or diver, belong to the family Gaviidae. Two, the Red-throated Loon *(Gavia stellata)* and the Arctic Loon *(G. arctica),* are circumpolar in their distribution. The former is the more widespread species, though both extend from the Arctic regions south to Scotland and, in the case of the former, to western Ireland. During the winter months both move south, and large flocks may sometimes gather in favorite bays.

The other species, the Common Loon *(G. immer)* and the Yellow-billed Loon *(G. adamsii),* are not as widespread. The former ranges over a large area of the northern United States and Canada, part of Greenland and Iceland. The latter occurs in northern Finland, east along the coasts of Russia and Siberia, Alaska and northern Canada. It does not seem to move very far south in winter and there are very few records of its occurring in Britain or other temperate European countries.

Common Eider (left) and Arctic Loon (right)

Several members of the waders, or shore birds as they are sometimes called, have some claim to being thought of as sea birds. The majority frequent the coast only during the off-season months, though some may breed on beaches, among sand dunes and in coastal marshes.

Two of the most unusual species are the sheathbills of the family Chionididae. These are the only birds with unwebbed feet which reach the shores of the Antarctic continent. They are found in large numbers on many islands in Antarctic waters, ranging from Tierra del Fuego and the Falklands eastward to those in the Indian Ocean. Pigeon-like in appearance, they have all-white plumage and pink eyes, with a peculiar yellow wattling on the cheeks, and thick-set, short, gray legs. The wings are short and have sharp spurs on the carpal joint that are used when the birds fight.

Although they are seen from time to time many hundreds of miles from land, most sheathbills spend their time along the shoreline, often scavenging near expedition bases. In the past every whaling station must have supported a large population of these birds. They will feed on any debris, decaying animal or vegetable matter that they can find. If none is available, they will eat any of the small marine animals along the shoreline. Around penguin colonies they are a particular menace, taking eggs and small chicks and picking up scraps of food left after the chicks are fed. One technique they have developed is for one of a pair to distract an adult penguin from feeding its chick by pecking at it, causing the penguin to drop the food, which the other sheathbill promptly snatches.

Although flocking together in large numbers, sheathbills tend to be more solitary when nesting. The normal nest site is among boulders, often close to a penguin colony. Two, sometimes three, eggs are laid. These take about 28 days to hatch, with both parents assisting in the incubation.

The chicks, covered in gray down at first, assume adult plumage before leaving the nest. During the winter months the southernmost population of these unusual birds moves northward, while those on the islands farther north are much more sedentary.

Sheathbill

BOOKS TO READ

Living Birds of the World. E. Thomas Gilliard. Doubleday, 1958. An excellent survey of the world's birds, including the various sea-bird groups.

Birds of the Antarctic. Edward A. Wilson. Humanities Press, 1967. A description of the birds that inhabit the Antarctic continent and islands adjacent to it.

Seabirds of the Tropical Atlantic Ocean. George E. Watson. Random House, 1966. The birds of such islands as the Cape Verdes and Ascension are discussed in detail.

Herring Gull's World. Niko Tinbergen. Doubleday, 1961. A classic account by one of the world's leading animal behavioralists.

Life Histories of North American Gulls and Terns. Arthur C. Bent. Dover, 1921. A volume dealing specifically with the family Laridae from Bent's famous 'life histories' series.

Galapagos, Island of Birds. Bryan Nelson. William Morrow, 1968. A study of the birds of an island which has fascinated biologists from Darwin's time to the present.

Birds of the Southwest Pacific. Ernst Mayr. Stechert-Hafner, 1945. A comprehensive account by a brilliant biologist.

Penguins. Bernard Stonehouse. Golden Press, 1968. A well-illustrated account of the various penguins from Emperors to Adelies.

Audubon Water Bird Guide. Richard H. Pough. Doubleday, 1951. An authoritative guide to the water, game and large land birds of eastern and central North America, including many of the sea-bird groups discussed in this text.

Bird Behavior. John Sparks. A Grosset All-Color Guide. Grosset & Dunlap, 1970. An authoritative, concise account of all aspects of the complex life of birds, including many sea bird species.

PLACES TO VISIT

Living sea birds can be seen at most large zoos, including the Bronx Zoo in New York, Chicago's Brookfield Zoo and the San Diego Zoo in California. Many sea birds, of course, especially gulls and terns, can be seen along the East, West and Gulf Coasts. Excellent dioramas showing sea birds in their natural habitats can be visited at such museums as the American Museum of Natural History, New York; United States National Museum, Washington, D.C.; Field Museum of Natural History, Chicago; and the Denver Museum of Natural History.

INDEX

Figures in bold type refer
to illustrations.

OTHER TITLES IN THE SERIES

The GROSSET ALL-COLOR GUIDES provide a library of authoritative information for readers of all ages. Each comprehensive text with its specially designed illustrations yields a unique insight into a particular area of man's interests and culture.